STORIES OF SOLIDARITY AND STRUGGLE

David Hinkley

STORIES OF SOLIDARITY AND STRUGGLE

A Life in the Worldwide Movement for Human Rights

The Activism and Social Movement Studies Collection

Collection Editor

R. Anna Hayward

LPp

I dedicate this work to all teachers, particularly to *al-Ustadh* Mahmoud Mohamed Taha of Sudan, Paulo Freire of Brazil, Catherine Walsh of Ireland, Hanan al Hroub of Palestine, and Emma Willard of the United States. Each exemplifies teachers who, in different places and times, set a transformative example of pedagogy that promotes both the transmission of knowledge and its application to the liberation of the individual, with the goal of freedom for every member of what Taha called "the human caravan".

First published in 2024 by Lived Places Publishing

British Library Cataloguing in Publication Data
A CIP record for this book is available from the British Library

ISBN: 9781916985933 (pbk)
ISBN: 9781916985957 (ePDF)
ISBN: 9781916985940 (ePUB)

Cover design by Fiachra McCarthy
Book design by Rachel Trolove of Twin Trail Design
Typeset by Newgen Publishing UK

Lived Places Publishing
Long Island
New York 11789

www.livedplacespublishing.com

Abstract

This memoir recollects true stories about the struggle for human rights, informed by the place of struggle lived in by each of the human rights champions you will meet here. While shaped by diverse cultural and political circumstances, threads of commonality link them all, because human rights and the voices defending them are universal. My grandmother and mother, who were teachers, taught me the meaning of solidarity—to stand with others and for principle, and to do what you can to make a difference. My journey starts there, where that consciousness began for me, and travels near and far. Welcome!

Key words

activism, Amnesty International, conscience, executions, Indigenous, movement, prisoners, solidarity, struggle

Contents

Introduction

In these pages, you will meet towering historical figures and ordinary people who share a passionate belief in human rights and the obligation of every human being to preserve, protect, and promote those rights. Because human rights are under continuous threat and attack throughout the world, these individuals decided—perhaps at first in the precincts of the heart—to do something. To act.

Each chapter tells a story of the struggle for human rights and human dignity over the past century, from Cherokee, Iowa to Khartoum, Sudan. What unites these stories is that, in ways large and small, each became a part of my life. I chose these memories from among many I collected on the long journey I have traveled because I believe each one may offer a useful model for activists in this century. I have included reflections on the methods and strategies employed in the campaigns and intercessions mounted by human rights organizations and individual advocates with whom I have collaborated, particularly during my long association with Amnesty International.

Learning objectives

- Assess the relevance of the human rights movement to issues and struggles you have experienced or encountered in your own life or community.
- Design an approach to applying the methods and strategies of human rights activism to struggles in your own life or community.
- Evaluate the changes in the mechanisms of achieving social change arising from twenty-first century advancements in research and communications.
- Investigate avenues of engagement in the human rights movement, identifying those that offer the most promise for application to struggles in your own life or community.
- Identify qualities shared by the human rights champions encountered here and qualities that distinguish them; consider which qualities and examples you personally find most inspiring or illuminating.

1
Mother in black and white: Inheritance and inspiration

Where, after all, do human rights begin? In small places, close to home—so close and so small that they cannot be seen on any maps of the world ... Such are the places where every man, woman and child seeks equal justice, equal opportunity, equal dignity without discrimination. Unless these rights have meaning there, they have little meaning anywhere.

— Eleanor Roosevelt, speech to the United Nations (quoted in *The New York Times*, March 28, 1958)

1925: Masked and unmasked

My mother was 13 when she, her younger brothers Philip and Billy, and Grandma Bowen walked from the old frontier Victorian on Walnut Street in Cherokee, Iowa, about a quarter mile down the hill to town. I suppose little Franny, three, was being looked after by one of the Shea aunts. Otherwise she was there too, probably being carried by Philip.

It was cold in late November 1925, but there was no snow yet. *The Phantom of the Opera* was showing at the Cherokee Opera House. After watching the Phantom creep up on poor Christine for 101 nerve-wracking minutes on a 20-foot-high screen, they trudged back up the hill by moonlight. I don't think Mother normally held Grandma's hand while they walked together, but that night she did.

Halfway home they saw a glow up ahead. They hurried to see, thinking somebody's house had caught fire. What they found was a mob in sheets and pointed hoods with eyeholes, some waving torches around, burning a cross on the front lawn of a Jewish physician and his family. Mother told me the doctor's name but I've forgotten it. There were no black people in Cherokee then, as far as I know, but the Klan had found somebody to hate.

Fresh from having their blood frozen by the Phantom's unmasking on the silver screen, here was a horror in three dimensions. Mother remembered being more appalled than terrified. Grandma Bowen, who took care of the children of a prominent local politician, suddenly recognized his wing tips under his robe. Still holding Mother's hand and with her boys in tow, she set her jaw, walked up to the Klansman, and said, "I love your kids, but don't ever bring them to me again."

1938: Get in the pool

Mother taught Physical Education at a combined elementary and high school in Elmhurst, a Chicago suburb, in 1938. Dad drove up from Eagle Grove, Iowa, often during the summer while she was getting situated and after that on some weekends. He bought her gifts, and they'd go dancing to big band music at one of the starlit ballrooms, drive the lakeshore and around town in his Ford, or, if Dad was lucky, in Grandpa's shiny black Buick Roadmaster. They'd have dinner and strudel at The Berghoff, an already old German restaurant in the Loop that Dad loved, having heard lore about it all his life. It was Grandpa Hinkley's favorite place for empire building, and the portions were legendary.

Fascism had been on the rise in Europe for 15 years. Hitler's invasion of Poland was only a year away. In America, Jim Crow laws were prevalent. By the time Mother moved there, Chicago had been enforcing racial segregation in public housing for a decade and would for years to come, long after the war began, Dad got drafted, and Mother returned to Iowa to teach in Fort Madison.

"Colored" water cooler in streetcar terminal, Oklahoma City, Oklahoma.

Photo credit: Russell Lee, July 7, 1939; public domain.

But at Elmhurst K-12, light was about to dawn. In early September, it was still warm enough to teach swimming for P.E. On the first day at the school pool, Mother found that all the black children just stood around while the white kids dove in, not waiting for Miss Bowen's instructions. She asked the black kids what they were waiting for. They pointed to the white kids. "Get in the pool," she said.

Four little words. Dozens of little faces instantly filled with doubt, confusion, and apprehension. But then, one tiny girl jumped in. Her friends, one by one, followed. In a moment Mother kept forever like a pressed flower in her memory, they were suddenly all in the water, splashing around. Cool water, pale blue like the sky. All of a sudden, something new. Everybody together. Sure, on the lakeshore, everybody was in the same water, but not on the same stretch of beach. And that was Lake Michigan, the size of a state. This was the school pool.

The girl who had led the way kept looking up at Mother. The afternoon sun backlit Mother's dark curls, ringing her pretty Irene Dunne-lookalike face. "You have a halo," the little girl said. A few white kids stared and pointed at the newcomers, whispered to each other, then swam to poolside, clambered onto the deck, and stood glaring at Mother, incredulous. "Get in the pool," Mother said. They did a double-take, trying to stare her down. When that didn't work, one shrugged and jumped back in. The others followed suit. They were different now than they would have been. Different for life. Maybe they even knew it.

Predictably, not long after, Mother was called into the principal's office. She was told the school had to be sensitive to the feelings and preferences of the parents. "Which ones?" she said.

The principal went beet red. "Why, for my part, of course I have no objection! But complaints have been lodged. You understand, don't you, Miss Bowen?"

"Hmm. Well, we're not going back to the old way now," Mother announced.

"No?" the principal said, sitting up straight, trying to stare her down.

"No," she said. "Imagine what the newspapers would think of that."

Mother at Elmhurst K-12 in 1938.

1961: You'd better

In 1961, I was a freshman in high school. Dinner was on the kitchen table. Dianne and Cathy were halfway finished. I was late. Mother's philosophy didn't have to be written down. It was in her eyes. You can sit down when you're ready to eat, but if your food is cold, too bad. Don't leave any on your plate. Over luke-warm pot roast and whole-kernel corn, I related a story I had just seen on the six o'clock news about a café in Oakland that "allegedly" turned away customers who were black. A sit-in had led to arrests. A protester was televised being dragged away, head bloody.

Mother listened, her face introspective and solemn. Dianne said Oakland was a crummy town and ought to be relocated to Mississippi or Alabama. Cathy thought she meant it literally and looked wounded for "Oaktown," a place we all liked, Cathy the animal lover most of all, because of Fairyland and the petting zoo. "Wasn't it just the one café?" she said. Dianne rolled her eyes. Cathy got it, laughed at herself, and put on her classic *omathon* (Irish for befuddled) face. "Oh. I thought that was a little drastic."

"They showed it all on the news," I said. "All the cops were white. If you ask me they put the wrong people in jail."

"Big surprise," Dianne said, leaving the table. Cathy followed, too late as usual. Whoever got to the den first got to choose what to watch on television. "First in!" was the cry of triumph, an absolute law at 3325 Cowper Street in Palo Alto. Mother cleared the table and then sat down while I finished my dinner. She poured me another glass of milk, and then in a faraway voice told me about the Phantom and the KKK in Cherokee, and about Jim Crow and the swimming pool in Elmhurst. I was always proud of Mother, unashamedly idolizing her all through my boyhood. Never more than right then, in the kitchen of our house, as the 1950s died and the 1960s struggled to be born. Mother finished her story and got started on the dishes. An *I Love Lucy* rerun, part of a marathon, could be heard down the hall, the plaintive echo of a show already long gone. Lucy and Ethel, Ricky and Fred on our black-and-white Sylvania, frequently punctuated by Dianne's giggle and Cathy's gigantic laugh. Mother stood at the sink with her back to me, rinsing and slipping the plates into the dishwasher. From then on, Mother's memories would be partly mine. I think she intended that. She was almost 50, Grandma Bowen had just died and those kids she taught P.E. in the 1930s now had kids of their own, going to school somewhere in America. "I want to do something, too, Mom," I said to her back.

"You'd better," she said without turning around.

2

Highlander: Music and struggle in the American South

> And he shall be like a tree planted by the rivers of water, that bringeth forth his fruit.
>
> —Psalm 1:3 and the inscription on Paul Tillich's gravestone
>
> Which side are you on?
>
> —Song title by labor rights activist Florence Reece, 1931

Death penalty abolitionists gather at Highlander

In 1979, when Larry Cox, Mike Jendrzejczyk, and I arrived at the Highlander Center in New Market, Tennessee, for a gathering of death penalty abolitionists, I knew almost nothing about the place or its storied history. But I liked the company I was in, the beauty of the Blue Ridge Mountains, and was looking forward to meeting kindred spirits from all over the South.

Most of the attendees were prison ministers from Tennessee, Georgia, Florida, and other Southern states, gearing up for impending executions. They knew the condemned as other pastors know members of their congregation who have confided their most shameful secrets in hopes of redemption.

Laughter and joking filled the main room when we got there, but looking at each face, I suddenly felt sad. Such good souls, yet etched into each face was the burden of knowing—knowing the terrible crimes of which the men and women they ministered to had been convicted, witnessing the wretched conditions and inhuman treatment endured on death row and knowing the grief and heartache of stricken families, both of the murder victims and the condemned.

A storm in the mountains

Discussions were stirring but without many glimmers of hope. So, I was glad on the second day when Tony Dunbar piled Larry, Mike, me, and an inflatable raft into his van and drove us to a nearby lake he knew. A brisk wind blew us quickly out to the center of the lake. Rain clouds formed up in minutes, heavy drops plummeted down, drenching us, and the Smoky Mountains suddenly boomed and rumbled. Oh yeah—mountain weather. Oops. The four of us tried paddling with all our strength, but the little raft was so overloaded that it made no headway in the stiffening wind. Lightning bolts kept striking the rod near the shoreline.

"Are we in trouble?" Mike yelled.

Tony laughed, nodding heartily. "Somebody's gotta get out and kick!" So there I was, in the middle of the lake, pushing the raft along, trying to avoid the churning paddles, glimpsing strikes on the lightning rod out of one watery eye, feeling the tingle and waiting for the big one that would turn me into a 200-pound roast puffer fish. I made eye contact with Larry's astonished face. He shook his head and laughed, and I laughed too, but underwater.

All the way back to Highlander in the van, the four of us took turns breaking out in laughter.

"Excellent idea, Tony," Larry mentioned.

"Wasn't it?" he grinned. "Shall we come back tomorrow?"

Walking in the footprints of history

On the final day of the conference, a private session was held, from which I was thoughtfully disinvited. A small group was planning civil disobedience. Today, Amnesty International policy approves of civil disobedience under its banner in specified circumstances and constraints and has published an online Civil Disobedience Toolkit, but in those years, Amnesty International prohibited its leaders and members from committing civil disobedience in Amnesty's name. As chairperson of Amnesty International USA's board of directors, I needed to be excluded from this discussion to protect Amnesty from any future charges of conspiracy. So I had time on my hands. I spent it roaming the grounds and talking to people who worked there about Highlander's history.

Maybe you know the feeling you sometimes get when you are walking in the footprints of history. I felt it at Highlander that day.

The events that distinguished its role in the labor movement and civil rights history occurred before the center was forced to move to its current location in New Market from its original site in Monteagle, Tennessee, but the footprints were there, pressed deeper into the path by the fidelity to the cause of all who carried it on.

In 2019, a white supremacist terrorist burned down much of the Highlander Center's HQ in Knoxville, a story that flickered on the news and was forgotten. I felt ashamed anew at how ignorant I was when I roamed those grounds myself. I had heard about the red-baiting that led to its shutdown by the State of Tennessee in 1961, and that Dr King, Rosa Parks, Pete Seeger, and others who gathered here had been hounded by J. Edgar Hoover's Federal Bureau of Investigation (FBI) in a futile effort to discredit them.

The first steps by its founders, of course, were taken in the marches of those who had gone before them. Their common spirit of solidarity with the oppressed and their belief in freedom led Myles Horton, Don West, and Jim Dombrowski, white Southern progressives, to found Highlander as a Folk School in 1932.

And the footprints lead farther back still, to Union Theological Seminary in Morningside Heights, New York City, where the words of Reinhold Niebuhr, Dietrich Bonhoeffer, and Paul Tillich had inspired Horton and Dombrowski. But the trail had really begun a century before in Denmark with Nikolai Frederik Severin Grundtvig, who created the movement for Danish Folk Schools. These schools set aside Latin and Greek and engaged students in learning about the world, the time, and the challenges all around them. Grundtvig convinced the Danish establishment democracy would be impossible without education that celebrates homegrown culture and involves young people in the life of the nation. "A tree planted by the rivers of water."

Preparing to teach junior high at St John Vianney School in East San Jose in 1972, I had studied Danish Folk Schools and tried applying similar principles within a Catholic K-8 double school, mostly without success. Irate parents demanded a return to textbook teaching. The principal caved. But I never forgot the excitement of my students when it was working. One usually jaded eighth-grader told me after an hour in a circle talking about differences each had experienced between law and justice, "First time I haven't once asked myself, why do I have to learn this?"

Music and community in the midst of struggle

Highlander's green lanes might have been quiet that evening, but for crickets and cicadas and a crackle in the air left over from the storm. I decided to go to my room and read, but magic stepped in. A guy who had come along as a second driver for one of the prison ministers stopped me. "You know the couple, the managing directors here?" he asked me.

"I met them."

"Did you know they're both bluegrass musicians?"

"No. You know them?" I wondered.

"No, I just heard it. I asked the husband if he'd play for the group. He said he was exhausted but maybe would ask her."

"Wow. That'd be great."

"Yeah, but he went home, and I think that's that."

"Maybe it's worth asking again," I suggested.

So, we walked the path through a pitch-dark stretch of woods to the directors' house. Dogs howled, and that was friendly compared to the expression on the tired director's face. His wife and co-director came out looking just as weary and skeptical but they came around instantly when we told them who they would be playing for. They knew the tireless effort prison ministers give day and night without fanfare or hope of earthly reward.

An hour later, the impromptu concert was well underway. Care and worries fell away in a merry parade of fiddle, banjo, dulcimer, autoharp, guitar, and washboard. In a mountain twang, the husband and wife sang old-timey tunes and folk ballads and played reels and railroad songs I had only heard on my grandma's radio as a child in Iowa. Weary legs rose and danced. Weary faces broke out in smiles. The music swelled, smiles turned to laughter. I so wished my wife Tina could be there, knowing she would be in heaven to the last note. The Almanac Singers' 1941 classic "Which Side Are You On" brought the house down. I thought of Pete Seeger, if he knew, smiling at this spontaneous, indelible moment. Likewise, Woody Guthrie, Leadbelly, Ramblin' Jack, and Cisco Houston, their souls still out there haunting the back roads and switching yards, singing the American story in the language of the people.

Joan Baez at the 1963 March on Washington.

Photo credit: USIA photographer; public domain.

In the music that rang on into the night, I heard, I think all of us heard, echoes of the music of revolt ringing through the decades, through the centuries, fanning the always-flickering flame of human freedom. I thought of Joan Baez, who, in 1973, had recruited me in the global fight for human rights and embodied for me the spirit of protest in song. I thought, too, of Cesar Chavez, Dolores Huerta and Bobby Kennedy. When did the United Farm Workers ever organize, march in protest, boycott and picket without music? It was while marching with them I learned most about music and struggle. I thought of Emma Goldman's immortal words: "If I can't dance, I don't want to be part of your revolution." Larry, Mike, and Tony came over to thank me for my part in bringing out the bluegrass. One quoted Friedrich Nietzsche, "Without music, life would be a mistake."

Looking back, moving forward

All these years later, every state in the South but Virginia still carries out executions. All the men and women who came to Highlander to prepare for a wave of state-sponsored killings have since then watched those in their spiritual care die, mostly of old age or suicide, on death rows throughout the region. Some, even after abolitionists' valiant and relentless efforts to turn away revenge disguised as justice, were electrocuted or poisoned by lethal injection. All of us watched as a global campaign to save Troy Davis, who had compelling evidence of his innocence, failed to prevent his shameful and tragic execution by the state of Georgia in 2011.

Along the way, many in our number have retired, some have passed away, including Mike Jendrzejczyk, our little brother. On the long drive back to New York in Rose Styron's borrowed Jeep wagon, hardly anything was said. We were going home, going back to work, with footprints of our own to leave as a trail for those who would follow.

Because, as everyone who takes up the cause of human rights and social justice learns, the path of struggle can only be taken by following in the footsteps of those who labored, struggled, most often failed, but persevered before you. Their work and worry must have seemed in vain more often than not. But they were bringing it to us, as we carried it to those who today lift new voices, from Ferguson, Missouri, to Khartoum, Sudan. Voices that will not be silenced, who will continue to fight for a better world, and to sing and dance to their own brave music.

3
Starke: The fight to stop an execution in Florida

Let anyone among you who is without sin be the first to cast a stone.

—John 8:7

The struggle for justice doesn't end with me. This struggle is for all the Troy Davises who came before me and all the ones who will come after.

—Troy Davis, quoted in Jealous, B. 'California Voters Should Remember Troy Davis This November', Huffington Post, September 20, 2016

An impending execution in Florida

In my long life, I have seen the best and the worst of my country. Sometimes, like one week in Florida in 1979, I found both in the same place at the same time.

It was my first visit to the state. It was springtime—hot and humid but with breezy mornings and evenings. Tallahassee is a pretty place for a government town, though I didn't get to see much of it. Within an hour of driving in from the airport, I was called to speak outside the governor's mansion. Amnesty International USA had sent me to help the legal defense team stop the impending executions of John Spenkelink and Willie Darden at Raiford State Prison in Starke, Florida. Larry Cox was there too, joining activists and prison ministers who were committing civil disobedience at the gates of the mansion.

John Spenkelink's mother, Lois, had come from California to plead for her son's life. She was suffering in the afternoon heat. Larry and others held signs over her to provide a little shade. She spoke with great difficulty to reporters, breathing heavily and fighting tears.

Foreground: Larry Cox, left, and me on the right at the protest outside the Florida Governor's Mansion before civil disobedience began, May 1979.

Photographer unknown; photo owned by me.

Scharlette Holdman was in charge. As the founder and direc-tor of the Florida Clearinghouse on Criminal Justice, she was assisting both Darden and Spenkelink's defense teams with late-stage constitutional challenges and the clemency appeal. Scharlette introduced me to Lois and led me to an intercom at the mansion gate. At her urging, I told Governor Graham's legal counsel that Amnesty International had come to plead for clemency and asked him to arrange a meeting for Lois with the governor.

"For what purpose?" he barked.

"To hear a mother's plea for her son's life. She has come—"

"The governor has already made his decision."

"I saw that, sir," I said. "Governor Graham says he's done everything his conscience requires. But he has not looked into the eyes of the mother of the man Florida is about to kill." I was grasping at something I had seen on local TV news during the few minutes I spent unpacking at my hotel before being rushed away. The lawyer's voice went up an octave. "Are you presuming to judge the governor's conscience?" he demanded. The outrage in his voice sounded practiced. I could almost see him winking at someone.

"No, sir, that's not my place, of course. I'm just saying this is something he may not have thought of before. Will you ask him, or are you making the decision for the governor?"

"I'm informing you of his decision. The answer is no."

I went with Scharlette to her office, where she told me what I needed to know about both death warrants. She was sure Willie Darden would get a stay but was worried about Spenkelink.

"They want to execute a white guy first," she said. "They want it real bad."

Finding a way to help

I asked her what I could do.

"We need a high-profile attorney to take the case to the Fifth Circuit and get a stay. Somebody they have to listen to. Ideally, somebody from the South."

"What about Ramsey Clark?" I wondered. Ramsey was a member of Amnesty's board. I knew him to be passionately opposed to executions; he had come to meetings when I needed his help during disputes about Amnesty's work for the abolition of the death penalty in the US.

Scharlette jumped at the prospect so I called Ramsey at his law office in New York and just caught him. He was about to head to Washington for hearings on the Strategic Arms Limitation Talks, Part II (SALT II) and disarmament. "I'll come," he said after some reflection. "That's a more important place for me to be. You're going to the Fifth Circuit, then? That's Judge Tuttle." I heard him sigh. "Yes, David, I'll come," he said again. "Seems like mine to do."

There had already been two executions since the US Supreme Court's Gregg v. Georgia decision of 1976 restored the death penalty after a four-year moratorium: Jesse Bishop and Gary Gilmore. They came first because each abandoned his legal appeals. Spenkelink and Darden were the first prisoners facing death warrants anywhere in the country who were fighting for commutation of their sentences to life without parole. Ramsey knew that once one "involuntary" execution was carried out the floodgates would open nationwide, especially in the South. He also knew he was the right one to take the Spenkelink appeal to the Fifth Circuit. He knew Judge Tuttle, knew he would get a fair hearing from him.

First, Ramsey flew to Tallahassee to be briefed by the defense team. Scharlette scheduled me to speak at a rally that afternoon at the state prison. Ramsey would join us there before heading to Atlanta and his presentation to the Circuit Court. I took some people with me in the rental car who knew the way. North Florida is table-flat, and you don't see much driving southeast on the interstate from Tallahassee to Raiford State Prison at Starke. Just south of the capital, though, back roads are green and dotted with wooded lakes and ponds all the way to the Gulf.

Reporters mobbed Ramsey, but he held them off until he was in front of the demonstrators so the cameras would show hundreds of people behind him with banners and placards. He waited still longer, slowly scanning the crowd and beyond us the growing throng of pro-death penalty revelers across a fire road the cops were using as a barrier. Finally, he began, "This is a sad day for our country…"

Getting Ramsey Clark to the Fifth Circuit Court of Appeals

After the statement and press interviews, I chauffeured Ramsey to Jacksonville to catch his flight to Atlanta. That's the drive

I remember best, though not for the scenery, pretty as it was. In New York, I never saw Ramsey Clark dressed in anything but a simple lawyerly dark suit and thin tie. Here he was dressed for the heat in white. In the car he shed the jacket and rolled up his sleeves. With the windows down and a warm wind blowing, we were quiet for a long time.

"This feels a little like back home," Ramsey reflected, watching farms and pecan groves whiz by. "The sky mostly. Puts me in mind of drives I took with Dad between Dallas and Sherman this time of year. Something sweet in the air." Quiet again. A pickup flying a small Confederate flag roared by. Ramsey shook his head. "Probably real nice boys," he said, "among their own." He told me about his father and grandfather, jurists and statesmen who revered the law. About his boyhood in Texas and how different it was coming back to it after the war. "Parts of our country change," he went on. "Others not so much. We travel not just through distance but through time, don't you think?"

Quiet again for a long time. I turned on the radio, promising to avoid news and talk shows. Eventually, I found a station playing country out of Jacksonville. Emmylou Harris was singing "Hickory Wind," a song I'd never heard. When she sang, "It's a hard way to find out that trouble is real..." something froze inside me. I didn't know what to make of it at that moment. Later, I realized it was foreboding.

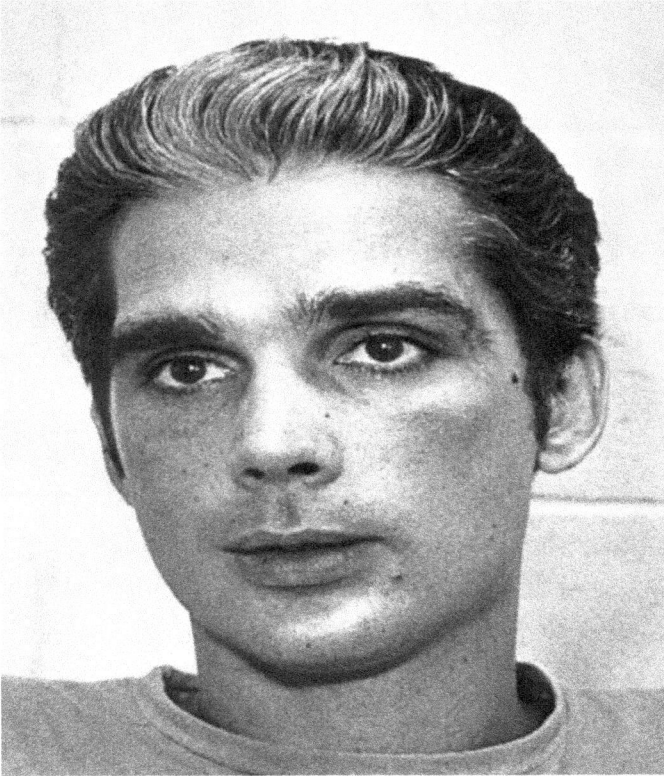

John Spenkelink, 1979. State Archives of Florida, Florida Memory.

Photo credit: Public domain.

"What are this kid's chances?" I asked Ramsey. His eyes were sad, introspective. "Judge Tuttle's a fine jurist," Ramsey sighed. "But David, he knows this Supreme Court and he has … a well-developed sense of futility."

"Oh. Not one of my gifts, I'm afraid," I admitted, taking his point. He smiled at me. For a moment, I wondered if he might be regretting his decision to come.

"Doesn't matter," he said. "We have to try."

"What about Willie Darden?" I asked as we neared the airport. He shook his head. "Not this time." Darden was reprieved that night but was executed in 1988 at age 54.

A trip back in time

On the drive back to Starke for the evening vigil outside death row, I took a little trip back in time myself, to the first thoughts I had ever had about the death penalty. In the spring of 1960, I was 13 years old, a seventh grader at Our Lady of the Rosary School in Palo Alto. Fifty restless baby boomers were crammed into our classroom, including 30 boys. It was a Catholic school with its image of discipline, but it was still the 1950s, and fistfights were frequent, with bullying an everyday nightmare for many. In religion class, we heard about the compassion, kindness, and strict nonviolence of early Christian communities. Nope. Step on my shoelace? Whap!

The playground was volatile, but the nuns ruled in the classroom, none with a steelier stare than our teacher and school principal, Sister Miriam David. As a teacher, Sister was earnest but uninspired, covering the material thoroughly and grading fairly but taking everything straight out of the textbook. A day could seem never to end. Nevertheless, I cherish three memories of Sister Miriam David.

On rainy days, she read to us. *Charlotte's Web* and *The Wind in the Willows* are two I remember, so young for us tweens but perfect, really. On some Fridays she switched on the radio for KDFC's presentation of operas condensed to their most iconic arias. *La*

Bohème, Madama Butterfly, Tosca, Turandot—I think Sister liked Puccini—are the ones I remember, but I looked forward to it, was always enchanted, and bless Sister for exposing me to some of the most beautiful music on Earth.

And on May 2, 1960, Sister Miriam David told us to bow our heads, fold our hands and be silent starting just before 10 a.m., when Caryl Chessman was scheduled to die in the gas chamber at San Quentin Prison less than 50 miles up Highway 101. Sister told us to pray not just for the soul of the condemned man but also for Governor Brown, who had denied Chessman clemency, and for ourselves and everyone in California, in whose name this was being done. She wove up and down the aisles, making sure we were all listening, our heads touching our desks.

"The Church teaches that the death penalty is wrong. To kill in cold blood is a mortal sin no matter who does it. Don't assume a law is always right. To protect a woman condemned under the law, Jesus said, 'Let him who is without sin cast the first stone.' No one is without sin, and no one has a right to take away what only God can give." The experience of waiting in silence while not far away a man was being deliberately killed has never completely left me. I feel deeply indebted to Sister Miriam David for this conscience-awakening moment.

Many years later, as western region director of Amnesty International USA, I asked former Governor Edmund G. "Pat" Brown to speak at a press conference in Sacramento when Amnesty released its report on capital punishment in the US. "What can I add?" he asked me.

"The voice of experience," I said. "Tell them about Chessman." Brown had spoken publicly about his regret at having caved under pressure to uphold the death sentence against Chessman even though he felt that the punishment was disproportionate to the crime. Chessman was convicted of aggravated rape and kidnapping. Adding kidnapping made it a capital crime at the time. The charge was based on moving his victim from one place to another; the "ransom" was money he stole from her purse. Chessman committed a terrible crime, but a death sentence was a travesty and a miscarriage of justice. At the press conference, Gov. Brown said, holding up his thumb, "No one should possess the power to lower his thumb and by doing so end the life of a human being."

A reprieve, an execution

Death penalty proponents always say it's for the most heinous crimes. That was not true of Chessman, and it wasn't true of John Spenkelink. Spenkelink was a drifter on a petty crime spree when a career criminal took over, according to Spenkelink terrorizing him and his friend. His friend testified that Spenkelink so feared and hated his tormentor he got a gun and shot the man in the back while he was asleep. Spenkelink refused a plea deal that would have meant a ten-year sentence, insisting it was self-defense.

On death row, Spenkelink was a model prisoner, helping developmentally disabled prisoners with their correspondence. He was so loved on death row that during our vigil, while we chanted, "Save John Spenkelink, close death row!" led by a local minister with a bullhorn, the inmates hung sheets out of their windows and set them aflame.

Late in the day, we got the stunning news that Ramsey Clark's efforts with Judge Tuttle had succeeded, leading in turn to a stay of execution for John Spenkelink ordered by Supreme Court Justice William Rehnquist. Many surrounded Lois Spenkelink, tears streaming. I said a few goodbyes and headed for Tallahassee and my flight back to New York.

The next day, I got a call from Larry Cox. Graham's lieutenant governor had rushed to Washington by private jet to get the stay lifted hours before Spenkelink's death warrant was set to expire. John Spenkelink was electrocuted the same day. I was at home in Putnam Lake, New York when I got the call. I remember walking around in a daze for a while, snatched back from euphoria to cold reality. I switched on the radio, and there it was as if providing a soundtrack for my memories: "Hickory Wind."

The work since then

In the years since then, I have been in Georgia on the Jack Potts case, in Louisiana for Colin Clark, and in Texas and Utah to discuss legislation. Here in California, at Scharlette Holdman's instigation, I was hired by the American Civil Liberties Union (ACLU) to assist the defense team in seeking clemency for Robert Harris in 1992. I was also brought on to help the defense team seeking clemency for Ray Allen in 2005. It was on that case I first worked closely with Denise Ferry, who has since become my editor on the Taha movie project and a dear friend.

In 2006, Michael Millman, executive director of the California Appellate Project (CAP), a specialized legal service funded by the State Supreme Court, hired me to co-author with him the clemency chapter of CAP's online manual for attorneys in capital case representation. Denise Ferry pitched in and was of indispensable help, as she always is.

Mike guided my research and worked with me on nearly every word. One of the great joys of my professional life was watching and listening to his keen intellect and Talmudic wisdom at work. Over the next four years, we literally wrote the book on executive clemency, completing it in March 2010. Fortunately, no capital case defense team has had any occasion to consult it because successive moratoria on executions have been imposed, the latest by Governor Newsom in 2019. Mike Millman didn't live to see Newsom's historic action, but he told me the last time we spoke in 2012 he was glad to have brought the manual into this century and that he was more hopeful than ever there would never be another execution in California.

Why this issue?

I have been asked many times why, of all human rights issues, I would devote so much of my life to trying, almost always unsuccessfully, to prevent convicted murderers from being executed for their crimes. Some of those asking were human rights activists who prefer to devote their energies to protecting the innocent and fighting for those persecuted for their beliefs. In this regard, it is worth noting that, according to the Death Penalty Information Center, "Since 1973, 200 former death-row prisoners

have been exonerated of all charges related to the wrongful con-
victions that had put them on death row."

It is easy for others to misunderstand, I think, what you are fighting for when you stand against the execution of people who
have been convicted of committing unspeakable crimes. Their
humanity and their rights as human beings are the beginning
and essence of it, as well as the possibility of their innocence.
But of course it isn't only for them. If you think a scheduled kill-
ing is wrong, you have to fight it. If you think it's an uncon-
scionable abuse of power every single time, you have to draw
the line and stand on it. From the moment a death warrant
is signed, if you are in a position to do something, silence is
complicity.

I'll admit this: it takes a lot out of you. The hatred in the eyes of
counter-protesters. Death threats and hate mail. Most heart-
wrenching of all, the scandalized stares of the grieving families of
murder victims. Some places you go thinking you'll pass through
and never return, only to find later on that part of you never
came home. Starke was one. This is a memoir, not a polemic, but
I'll say this much here: we allow the noose and the lynch mob in
our democracy at our peril and to our everlasting shame.

I have seen the best of our country and the worst. Against a
monstrosity draped in the color of law stands a small but heroic
network of dedicated lawyers, writers, researchers, specialists,
organizers and activists, prison ministers and inmates' families,
and abolitionist organizations like Death Penalty Action, Death
Penalty Focus, the ACLU and Amnesty International.

Their largely unsung achievements and brilliant, tireless work hasten the slow-coming dawn when we can close death row for good and dump all poison syringes, electric chairs, gallows and gas chambers on the scrapheap of history with the slave block and torture rack. I swear on that day my soul, wherever it may be, and the spirit of our country will soar.

4
A threnody for Lilian Ngoyi: South Africa under apartheid

When the true history of South Africa is written, Lilian Ngoyi's name will appear in letters of gold.

—Archbishop Desmond Tutu, eulogy at her funeral, quoted by Martha Evans in The Conversation, 2022

My first experience of diplomacy

In the spring of 1980, Amnesty International USA board member Barbara Sproul invited me to attend a memorial service for Lilian Ngoyi of South Africa, held at the chapel of the United Nations Church Center in New York. The gathering was unlike any other I have ever attended, and the memory of it has never left me.

For many of us active in the human rights movement in the 1970s and 1980s, solidarity actions and intercessions for political prisoners in South Africa were consistently high priorities. I never played a leadership role in the struggle, but in 1979, as chairperson of Amnesty USA's board of directors, it was my duty to meet with the South African Ambassador to the United States when Amnesty received an unexpected request from him for a meeting at the embassy. It was to be the occasion for my first and only advocacy on behalf of Lilian's case during her lifetime.

For the first ten minutes of our meeting, an incensed Ambassador Donald Bell Sole upbraided me for Amnesty's appointment of Derek Roebuck, a former member of the Communist Party in Australia, to the post of Head of Research. In a just-published *New York Times* editorial, the appointment had been deemed "injudicious". The diplomatic invitation followed almost immediately, so it was not really a surprise when Sole greeted me with the editorial in hand and a diatribe on the subject. I didn't try to interrupt as he went on, leaning across the table between us and pointing at my nose to mock the moral posturing of American critics of his nation, "You who look down your long noses from the land of Jim Crow!"

When he finally took a breath, I said I had no comment on decisions made at the Secretariat, that I was also not there to represent the US government of the past or present, but eagerly welcomed the rare opportunity to benefit from a meeting of minds between his office and Amnesty. I clarified that I had come to discuss human rights violations such as arbitrary arrests, detention without trial, and the use of banning orders. He snorted, literally. I thought it best to ignore that and asked how he responded to criticism of banning orders in particular as being cruel, petty and of no demonstrable necessity.

Banning orders, imposed in South Africa between 1950 and 1990, confined more than 2,000 people for extended and renewable

periods to their homes or immediate surroundings and prohibited them from meeting with more than one person at a time
(other than family). These orders also forced them to resign any
offices in any organization, prohibited them from speaking publicly or writing for any publication, and barred them from certain
areas, buildings, and institutions.

Sole stared at me in silence. A stone face. OK. I kept moving the
"conversation" toward the specifics in the material I had brought.
Eventually, I asked the ambassador about prisoners of conscience
adopted by local chapters in the US section. My final question
was about the imposition of a third consecutive five-year banning order on Lilian Ngoyi. "How shall I report Your Excellency's
view of the continued imposition of a third banning order on
Lilian Ngoyi, a woman now in her sixties who self-evidently poses
no credible threat to South African national security?"

Not a word. Maybe a yawn, or perhaps I just saw a yawn in
his eyes. I tapped the paperwork. "A suggestion from you that
Lilian Ngoyi has endured enough could end this ordeal for her.
Internationally, it would be seen as a reflection of openness to
constructive dialogue. I hope you will personally consider all
these cases as part of a recalibration of proportionality in the
administration of justice."

Ambassador Sole had abruptly dropped the ire and replaced it
with ennui as soon as I started talking about specific cases. He
looked over the paperwork I brought and said he had "nothing
to add". I thought then and still suspect he was relieved to find
I was not going to lecture him about the apartheid system itself.
Sole had a scowl right out of central casting. I didn't get to see his

version of a smile until we parted, nodding at the door but without shaking hands. I think his smile was genuine, to the extent that he was glad to be seeing the last of me, but I took a long second before turning away to give him the unflinching stare I thought would represent Lilian and the other prisoners of conscience best.

Activism in New York City creates a lifeline and a platform

Even before that audience at the embassy, I had become aware of the personal activism of Barbara Sproul and the tireless efforts of her local Amnesty group in New York City on Lilian Ngoyi's behalf. Besides regular correspondence that formed a lifeline for Lilian to the world outside South Africa, Prof. Sproul, head of the religion program at New York's Hunter College, arranged to have some of Lilian's letters printed as an anonymous op-ed in the New York Times on May 6, 1978.

As a result of the op-ed's appearance, in spite of everything the South African government had been doing for 15 years to silence Lilian Ngoyi, her powerful voice was heard after all. Under the title, "It Is Not God Who Made Apartheid" and with the byline "A South African," she began her first letter, "In this awful time of trial, it is a great help to know that friends are thinking of us as Human Beings."

The Riverside Drive, New York City, Amnesty group began working for Lilian Ngoyi in 1966, a year before her second banning order was imposed, and persevered until her death in 1980. At the chapel for her memorial, I felt their grief, as I expected to.

I came feeling deeply honored by the opportunity to mourn her alongside many who had long labored to win her freedom. Even so, I was completely unprepared for the powerful emotional impact of her memorial.

The words spoken there, in particular by Reverend William Sloane Coffin, were passionate and eloquent. But it was above all the musical tribute to Lilian by South African composer, musician and vocalist Hugh Masekela that seared the moment into every soul present. In his threnody—a lamentation in verse or song— he played long, arching notes on his trumpet that seemed to swirl around the chapel walls and return, return, return. Then he chanted her name, sending it soaring so high you could feel him trying to make Lilian hear it somehow. Some present had to steady themselves. Some wept. I know that the words I offer cannot do Lilian Ngoyi justice. But I think the threnody that was offered that day was worthy even of her.

Lilian Ngoyi and the epoch-making changes she witnessed

Lilian Masediba Ngoyi, born in 1911, was the only daughter of a washerwoman and domestic worker and a laborer who became disabled and eventually died of a mining-related disease. A mother by the age of 20, Lilian became a widow at 26. Obligations multiplied. She spent the next decade caring for her own son, her brother's child after the death of her brother's wife, and her elderly parents. They lived in poverty in The Shelters, site of South Africa's first urban land invasion and the proving ground for what was to become the South West Townships—Soweto.

While eking out a living there, Lilian witnessed the epoch-making events that would change her country forever.

First came the National Party (NP) in 1948, which provoked an immediate backlash and ever-intensifying suppression of the rights, movement, political and civil society participation of all non-whites by the Afrikaner government. These cruel and humiliating impositions in turn galvanized a new generation of leadership in the African National Congress (ANC). Walter Sisulu, Oliver Tambo, and Nelson Mandela orchestrated an escalation of ANC resistance tactics including civil disobedience, boycotts, and strikes, culminating in the Defiance Campaign of 1952.

On June 26 of that year, 52 Africans and Indians, including Nelson Mandela, marched without permits into Boksburg, near Johannesburg, and were immediately arrested. In Port Elizabeth, 30 "defiers" were jailed after entering a railway station through the "Europeans Only" entrance. Hundreds more were picked up in the weeks to follow for participating in a broad range of organized and spontaneous anti-apartheid actions, including entering the "European" sections of public buildings or sitting on benches marked for whites. After each mass arrest, more defiers joined the campaign. By 1953, over 8,000 had been arrested for defying the NP government's strict enforcement of racial segregation policies. At first, most of those arrested served relatively brief sentences or paid fines. However, as the protests spread to other parts of South Africa and thousands of new members joined the Defiance Campaign and the ranks of the ANC, the government cracked down. Sentences grew harsher. Reports of ill treatment in detention multiplied.

Lilian at the crossroads of history

For Lilian Ngoyi, the Defiance Campaign was a crossroads. Now 42 years old, her circumstances already difficult, Lilian knew joining the campaign meant risking the loss of her factory position and the horrifying prospect of a three-year sentence in a South African prison.

If you have ever faced a transformative decision in your own journey, you may be able to imagine that moment in Lilian Ngoyi's life: the worrying, contemplating the stakes for herself and those she loved, all the dire consequences of taking action writ large in headlines and no doubt repeated in somber conversations among the people in her community. For my part, ever since that mournful but beautiful memorial gathering in New York, I sometimes picture her preparing herself on that morning in 1953 for the day ahead—a day of personal destiny. What to wear. What to put away. What to pass to neighbors so it wouldn't spoil or go to waste.

Perhaps with a few deep breaths as she walks, she makes her way to the building that forms her personal point of no return. There, by the simple act of walking into the whites-only section of a Johannesburg post office, alone, Lilian places her feet on the path of history. As she must have known they would, those few steps would change her life forever. Steps that had to be taken alone but which connected hers to footprints pressed into the path of struggle everywhere, in every age.

In the aftermath of her protest in the Defiance Campaign, Lilian joined the ANC, quickly rising to leadership roles. She also joined

Fedsaw, the Federation of South African Women, where she met and forged a lifelong friendship with trade unionist Helen Joseph.

In 1955, Ngoyi was sponsored for an overseas trip by the Women's International Democratic Federation, attending conferences in Europe, China, and the USSR. The experience of being treated with respect renewed her energy, and the opportunities to showcase and develop her skills as a speaker prepared her for a greater leadership role in the work she took up upon her return.

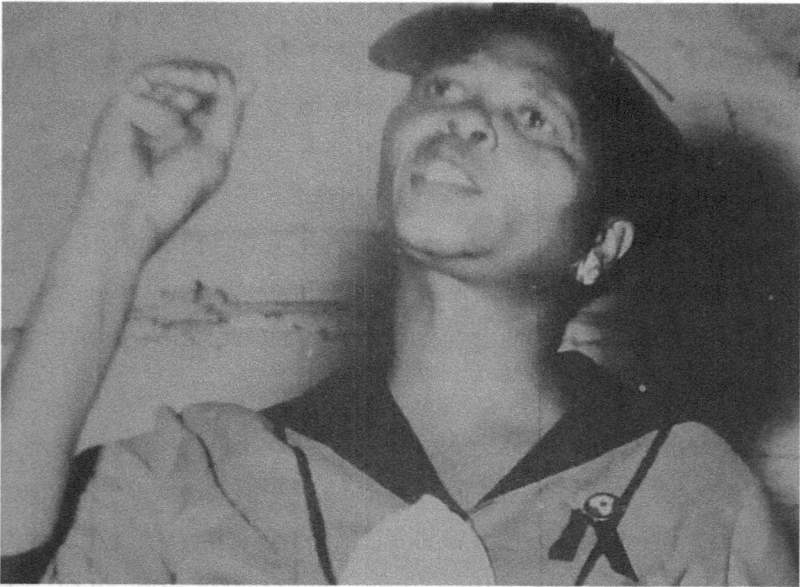

Lilian Ngoyi making a speech in 1960.

Photo credit: Azola Daniel/Wikimedia Commons, SA.

In the wake of the government's extension to women of the notorious "pass laws"—imposed to facilitate government monitoring and control of the freedom of movement of all non-whites—a coalition of women's organizations under Fedsaw's umbrella set out to organize the largest gathering of women in South African history.

On August 9, 1956, now commemorated as Women's Day in South Africa, Lilian Ngoyi and Helen Joseph led an estimated 20,000 women to the Union Buildings in Pretoria. The size and passion of the march and its fearless oratory stunned the government and stimulated anti-apartheid activism throughout the country and internationally. Lilian herself became a widely known and beloved figure, affectionately called by her admirers Ma-Ngoyi.

Lilian is imprisoned and subjected to banning orders

A 2022 article by Martha Evans in The Conversation, which has provided me with historical background for this chapter, concluded its summary of her role in history after the march with the following paragraphs.

"In 1956, Lilian Ngoyi was among 156 dissidents arrested in a swoop by security police. Charged with treason, they became known as the Treason Trialists. She was finally acquitted in 1960, but had lost her job as a factory machinist. She was soon arrested again and detained for five months, 19 days of which she spent in solitary confinement. In a 1963 arrest, she spent 71 days in solitary, an experience that affected her ability to focus.

"Thereafter, Ngoyi drops out of history. She was subjected to three five-year banning orders, living in a state of permanent lockdown. For most of the remainder of her life she was forbidden from interacting with other banned persons. She was unable to meet with more than three people at a time and could not attend a lecture, go to the cinema, or accept invitations to weddings, funerals or parties of any sort.

"The banning orders ended her political career and gradually eroded her ability to earn a living as a seamstress, unable to travel into town to purchase fabrics. Security police frequently raided her home, chasing away potential customers. Ngoyi was forced to rely on sporadic donations.

"In a letter of gratitude to a sponsor, she expressed the humiliation of her position:

We feel small to say thanks all the time.

"Not the wife of an elite ANC leader, she received no financial contributions from exiled men, nor was she supported by the International Defence and Aid Fund, which helped the families of political prisoners. She did not lose hope, however, and, like Mandela, took solace in gardening, planting seeds sent to her by her overseas friends. Her small yard was full of blooms.

"On 13 March 1980, two months before her third banning order was due to expire, Ngoyi passed away, aged 69. She never saw freedom in her lifetime, nor did she receive the recognition she deserved for her efforts to achieve it. At her funeral, activist and church leader Desmond Tutu said that when the true history of South Africa was written, Ngoyi's name would be in 'letters of gold'.

"This has manifested to some extent—a few clinics and roads bear her name. But the true nature of her accomplishments and challenges, and those of other banned and banished persons in South Africa, should never be forgotten."

Enduring solidarity and the recognition of history

Barbara Sproul saw the Lilian Ngoyi Clinic in Johannesburg when she visited Lilian's home in Soweto. After all these years, Barbara is still in touch with Lilian's family, a reflection of how personal the ties can become and how long they can endure between Amnesty activists and the prisoners and prisoners' families they work to assist.

On a sad spring day in 1980 in New York City, Barbara and other activists who had come to love and admire Lilian Ngoyi, while struggling over many years to free her, listened in silence as Hugh Masekela played and chanted a threnody in her name—her beautiful name—at her memorial. I can't find the words to describe it, but I have never heard love, admiration, and sorrow inhabit a passage of music more vividly in my life.

There currently exists no biography of Lilian Ngoyi, whose personal witness and irreplaceable contributions to the struggle to end apartheid cry out for the recognition of history. However, I have just learned that historian Martha Evans is developing a biography of Lilian, scheduled to be published by Penguin Random House in 2025. For me, this is thrilling news. The threnody for Lilian Ngoyi that still echoes in the hearts of all who mourn her passing should not be the last sound heard by the world of her inspiring story.

5
Rimini: Friendship, solidarity and the defense of Indigenous rights in the Americas

Ships that pass in the night, and speak each other in passing, only a signal shown, and a distant voice in the darkness; So on the ocean of life, we pass and speak one another, only a look and a voice, then darkness again and a silence.

—Henry Wadsworth Longfellow, *Tales of a Wayside Inn*, 1863

Friendship and solidarity

Friendships, I have found, the dearest most of all, cannot be put into words. The bonds we form are ineluctable; attempting to illuminate them is hopeless work. In these pages I have recollected some moments friends and I have shared, doing my best to honor their words and actions and pay only such compliments as my heart compels. But I haven't tried to and couldn't express what they mean to me.

At an Amnesty gathering in Cambridge, England, in 1978, I was captivated from a distance by a small group of friends from Amnesty Italy. The first thing I noticed was that among many clusters of delegates from 50 countries scattered around the halls and cafés of the venerable university town, the Italians were the only ones singing. I noticed a bottle of grappa going around, hand to hand, and drifted toward their corner.

I might otherwise have headed to my room brutally jetlagged and existentially disappointed after a long day of confronting entrenched retrograde thinking and fear of change in one policy debate after another. The last thing I wanted was to find myself in one of the clusters where the same arguments raged merrily on. Just in time I heard the jubilant strains of *"Funiculi, funicula!"* punctuated by laughter. I can still hear it. I can still see their faces, see their eyes sparkle as they listened to and teased each other. I have only to close my eyes and I can still hear them talking and laughing, one and all: Cesare, Amedeo, Michele, Antonio, and Franca.

Cesare Pogliano, president of Amnesty Italy, was a man quite serious about serious matters but about all else a hilarious wag, for me like one of Fellini's clowns but without makeup or prat-falls. It was impossible to remain upset or unhappy in his company. Once, when he saw me gritting my teeth and shaking my head in exasperation after a chaotic working party descended into rancor, he shook his head, ran up and leapt into my arms, demanding, "I must see you smile, or else!"

"You win. I've missed you," I told him, smiling.

"Impossible!" he assured me.

Cesare passed away many years ago, tragically, too young, but he was right about my missing him after all. There is still a glow in my heart that belongs just to him, so he is never far away.

Amedeo is in there too, with his soft heart, generous mind and deep appreciation of all good things. In Helsinki, as my final term as council chairperson ended, I meant to recognize Amedeo, who had prepared a goodbye message to me on behalf of the council, but I could not find him in the crowd and another delegate rose to thank me. Amedeo was so disappointed he wept, and I have always regretted not searching longer for him, but he gave me his words with a tearful hug later and I remember their warmth and kindness were straight from the giant teddy bear heart of Amedeo Flachi.

Michelangelo Mosca, our Michele, also gone from this world far too young, was as warm as his big smile and the pasta he served us in the caravan we all hung out in. Quiet and thoughtful, he seemed to carry within and bring the sun of Southern Italy into every room.

Antonio Marchesi, now chairman of Amnesty International Italy and a distinguished professor of international law at the American University of Rome, was in those days our handsome little brother. Though more than 40 years have passed, I can still only imagine him young, wise beyond his years and such fun. He brought youth and willing hands and never missed a thing.

Franca's birthday. Franca on my right, Cesare standing at left, Antonio standing at right.

Photo credit: Michelangelo Mosca; used by permission of its owner, Amedeo Flachi, seated second from right.

And at the center of our little troupe was Franca Sciuto. From that first evening in Cambridge, Franca entered my mind and heart deeply, suddenly, mysteriously. In her eyes, I saw a serious, brilliant mind and a deeply sorrowful but indomitable soul. Her sad, often sardonic but irrepressible smile evoked for me Giulietta Massina, who had long before captured my heart in films like *La Strada* and *Nights of Cabiria*. Like Giulietta, Franca seemed to be carrying a great weight within. I have never felt I could alleviate that burden in any way and therefore have never tried. The weight has become much, much heavier in the years I've known her, most crushingly because of the death in an accident of her beloved daughter. There are no words for such a loss. Yet she soldiers on, to me an evergreen inspiration and a precious treasure. She is never far from my thoughts, to this day.

Rimini, Italy, in 1982, was where we first gathered in the caravan, all together. I don't remember anything that was said there. Other friends joined us there from time to time, including former Prisoners of Conscience and Amnesty USA board members Juan Méndez, an attorney from Argentina, and Vinny McGee, who'd been imprisoned in the US for resisting the draft during the war in Vietnam. Vinny and Juan joined Franca and me for a memorable drive down the Appian Way to Rome after the council that year. When crowded with friends, chatter and hilarity filled the caravan. But most often it was just a few of us around the table with wine, coffee and food. We made each other laugh and without many words being said grew close and happy, one and all, to be together. Unlike other Amnesty friends and colleagues I spent time with at councils, our troupe never spoke about the issues under debate. Our common purpose in the human rights movement was understood and seemed not to come into it at those moments. Our time together was for each other.

An issue that binds us still: The rights of Indigenous peoples

But issues have also bound us, especially Franca and me, over the years. A shared concern for the rights of Indigenous peoples in particular has more than once brought us together. It led me to accept directorship of Survival International in the US for a time, while Franca has done much more, becoming a driving force in the Rainforest Foundation, for some years directed by our mutual friend Larry Cox, and subsequently the Rainforest Fund. Over the years I have kept in touch by letter and email, and have followed her great work with deep admiration.

My own involvement in the struggle for Indigenous peoples' rights began early in my adult life and continues today. In 1968, while my wife Tina and I were living in married student housing at San Francisco State, we became acquainted and for a time friends with Pat Geneeha, Richard Oakes and other Native American activists who lived and studied there. Knowing them, seeing them spied on, jailed and harassed, witnessing their courage and resolve, brought the Trail of Tears—the genocide of Indigenous peoples living here—right to our doorstep and into our home. The tragic death of Richard's child in a fall during the Alcatraz takeover and then his murder were shocks that hit Tina and me hard and still hurt half a century later. After knowing Richard and a few of his friends, the issue became personal for me in a way I can neither express nor ever forget.

The Aché of Paraguay

I suppose that's why, when Marketa Freund, Amnesty USA country coordinator for Paraguay, called me in 1978 to ask that I champion the cause of the Aché and Moro peoples at an upcoming Amnesty Council, I knew at once I had to try. It would not be easy, I knew. Amnesty International had up to then never become involved in the struggle to protect Indigenous peoples and defend their rights. Asking around after my talk with

Marketa, I found little support for the idea. There were other organizations in that fight, notably Cultural Survival and Survival International (SI).

The year before SI had sent anthropologist Richard Arens to Paraguay to investigate, and it was his report that had mobilized Marketa. But Arens's research was under intense scrutiny and had already drawn fire for alleged sensationalism and superficiality. Most friends and colleagues discouraged me from taking it on. So I called Dr Arens and talked it over with him for nearly an hour. He was defensive, sounding sick of questions he must have been hearing a lot. But when he got going, the heart of the matter began to come into focus. It wasn't just about forced sedentarization of nomadic forest peoples, a phrase that can mask in academic language the suffering of real human beings.

Dr Arens talked about the Aché he met and got to know in his month's sojourn. Aché mothers and fathers whose deprivation was so stark they put their children in bonded servitude to landed families just to save them from starvation. A father who risked arrest to get a peek at his little sons working in a rich man's field, and was beaten for it. For a moment, Arens stopped. I could hear tears in his voice as he tried to continue. "I'll see what I can do," I told him, and let him go.

So I did my best. After gathering support in the US section at regional conferences and the annual meeting, at a working party at the next International Council Meeting, in Louvain, Belgium, I stood up and made a speech defending a policy resolution calling upon Amnesty's research department to investigate the circumstances of the Aché. I don't remember my speech. I know I expressed understanding of the difficulty for Amnesty, accustomed as it was to acting on specific information about named individuals, often presented by family members, attorneys, and other sources whose allegations can be independently checked. But I argued that habits of methodology should not prevent Amnesty from recognizing that the Aché's inhuman treatment fell squarely within its mandate, which called for assisting people who were imprisoned or *otherwise physically restricted* because of their beliefs, their race, religion, language, or ethnic origin.

In 1979, Amnesty was not ready to enter the struggle to defend Indigenous rights

The resolution failed, but in the discussion I heard heartfelt testimony from leaders in several Latin American Amnesty sections, including some who were witnessing similar treatment of Indigenous people in their countries. A compromise was reached leaving the matter to the International Executive Committee. Facing vigorous opposition from Amnesty's Secretary General and encouraged to stay out of it by nongovernmental organizations (NGOs) in the field, Amnesty never took action for the Aché.

Later, I learned that Franca Sciuto was at that working party in Louvain. She told me she had been moved by my speech and never forgot it. It may even have provided a spark that she has fanned into a flame of a passionate commitment over the ensuing four decades.

Marketa Freund, profoundly disappointed by the Council's demurral, found ways to fight for the Aché of Paraguay through her own network. It was reportedly said of her by activists in at least two South American countries that if Marketa was on your side when you landed in prison, you'd eventually be set free. Recruiting Marketa and arranging Amnesty funding for her work and that of her mother, Henriette Horenovsky—brilliant women who had survived Nazi concentration camps in their native Czechoslovakia and who devoted their lives to human rights—was one of my most enduring contributions to the cause.

I think of Marketa and Henriette often these days, I suppose because of the Costa Rica work I am involved in now. I see them in their little house in Boulder, incessantly abuzz with phone traffic, hard to navigate through mounds of mail and new dossiers that endlessly patient Henriette sorted while Marketa pecked and criticized. But how they loved each other! Marketa called her mother *"Nufi,"* always with the slightest echo of childhood in her voice, melting my heart. I'm happy to say some generous Amnesty friends took care of them in their last years, when both suffered cognitive decline and health troubles, until they passed away. No one deserved such kindness more.

Amnesty enters the fight

In 1979, Amnesty was not prepared to enter the struggle for Indigenous rights. Today, that has changed. In 2007, when

Amnesty USA executive director Larry Cox put me in charge of campaigns in an interim executive role, I learned that Amnesty had just released a new report titled "Maze of Injustice: The Failure to Protect Indigenous Women from Sexual Violence in the USA." Nearly 30 years after the Louvain demurral, Amnesty had found a way to contribute without leaving its standing or changing its mandate.

The Bribri and Brörán of Costa Rica

In 2019, the struggle for Indigenous peoples' defense brought Franca and me together again. At her request and with her guidance, I have been collaborating with attorneys Vanessa Jimenez and Nathalia Ulloa of the Forest Peoples Programme (UK) in an effort to protect the Bribri and Brörán of Costa Rica from murderous assaults carried out with impunity by private forces trying to drive them from their legally designated ancestral lands.

People accustomed to thinking of Costa Rica as a forest paradise and a bastion of democracy and human rights in the region would be shocked and alarmed at the persistent failure of the government to enforce the laws meant to protect the rights and safety of Indigenous people in those magnificent forests. Of the four Indigenous leaders granted special protections by the Inter-American Commission on Human Rights (IACHR), beginning when threats and assaults mounted in 2012, two have been murdered.

Pablo Sivas Sivas.

Photo credit: Dr Francisco Javier Mojica Mendieta; used by permission of the photographer.

Sergio Rojas Ortiz was murdered in his home in 2019; the case was officially closed in 2022 without an arrest. Mainor Ortiz Delgado was shot and badly wounded in 2020; he's been subjected to multiple death threats and an arson attack on his home; no meaningful investigation has been undertaken. Pablo Sivas Sivas has also been subjected to nearly continuous threats of violence for over a decade; his home was burned down in 2020; yet there have been no arrests in any of these cases

Jehry Rivera Rivera was shot to death during a mob attack on Indigenous families in the presence of many police officers in 2020. Thanks to a pregnant mother's courageous identification of Rivera's assassin, Juan Varela Rojas was arrested, tried and sentenced to 20 to 22 years in prison in 2023. The conviction of a non-Indigenous defendant for the murder of an Indigenous person is certainly an extreme rarity and may even be a historical first in Costa Rica.

Since Franca called on me to help in the work for the Bribri and Brörán, I've been doing what I can. The Costa Rican government has responded to my inquiries with incomplete and misleading information, but the door to a dialogue is ajar and we'll see what persistence can achieve. The coronavirus pandemic has complicated this endeavor like all others, but must not be allowed to become a veil concealing further assaults and continued government inaction. The work, as always, goes on. And, as in bygone days, even such challenging and often heartbreaking work bestows its own joy in such inspiring and beloved company.

Amedeo sent Easter greetings this spring, eliciting warm replies from Antonio, Franca and me. In her closing, Franca wrote, *"Siete tutti nel mio cuore."* ("You are all in my heart.")

Grazie, Franca. E anche il mio. (Mine too.)

Cesare, Franca and me in the caravan.

Photo credit: Michelangelo Mosca, used by permission of its owner, Amedeo Flachi.

6

Carla Cristi: Pinochet threatens Chilean artists

We can live with lots of things, but we can't live without imagination, we can't live without hope.

—Ariel Dorfman (2011) in an interview on the Tavis Smiley Show, PBS

Gracias a la vida.

—Violeta Parra (1966). The title of her song

Fascism comes to Chile

In June 1973, Joan Baez and Ginetta Sagan introduced me to Amnesty International. Ginetta, a courier for the anti-Fascist underground in Italy during the Second World War, had been imprisoned and tortured by the Nazis. After the war, she continued to devote herself to the human rights struggle. Joan and Ginetta worked feverishly all that summer with former prisoner of conscience Lady Amalia Fleming to expose and end the torture of prisoners in Greece under the Papadopoulos regime, finally taking a breath when a general amnesty was declared in August. I did what I could, learning the work along the way.

"Fascism didn't end with Nazi Germany, of course," Ginetta said one warm evening in a weary voice at the kitchen table of her Atherton, California home. "The Colonels will fall. They must. But it will not stop there either," she sighed. A month later, it came to Chile.

Ginetta Moroni Sagan. Recipient of the 1996 Presidential Medal of Freedom.

Photo credit: Wikimedia, public domain.

During that first year of teaching eighth-grade social studies, math, and science at St John Vianney School in East San Jose, I had found trying to interest junior high students in history and civics a daily challenge. Debates helped. Taking positions awakened their feelings and got them talking to each other. From a list of issues, I let them choose one topic each month. For the last debate, two students proposed one that was not on the list: President Salvador Allende's nationalization of copper mining in Chile. A few weeks before, one of my eighth graders had introduced the subject during "current events," our Friday selection of news stories. After that she became a big fan of Allende. She had already written quite original and beautifully hand-illustrated reports on Zapata, Sandino, Che Guevara, and Frida Kahlo but announced, "Now I like Salvador best because he's alive." I said OK if she could recruit a partner and a team to take the opposing position. She and another free-thinker took Allende's side. Two clever boys who ran a mail-order sports collectibles operation from home that already brought in more than my salary spoke for Anaconda and Kennecott Copper corporations and communications giant ITT. I remember our panel of nine student judges awarded the debate, in their words, to "Allende, all the way." A few weeks after the debate, while driving home to Los Gatos I heard Joan Baez talking about Amnesty International on rock radio station KLIV. I had never heard of Amnesty, but the next day I called the number. It was Ginetta Sagan's home phone. Joan answered and we talked, then Ginetta took the phone and urged me to come over at once. Steps onto a path I have traveled ever since.

Ginetta took advantage of positive developments in Greece to work on prisoner of conscience cases in Iran, South Africa and Uruguay, among others. I started working for the release of Ismael Bakri, sentenced to life for being a communist in Indonesia, and Aleksandr Feldman, jailed for not being a communist in the USSR.

Meanwhile, in Chile, two years of overt and covert efforts by the Nixon administration and its corporate cronies, including leading an international boycott of Chilean goods and financing a truckers' strike, had crippled the economy. Then, with US government encouragement and Central Intelligence Agency (CIA) complicity, Gen. Augusto Pinochet seized power in a bloody military coup on September 11, 1973.

The human cost of Pinochet's junta

Thousands were detained in the soccer stadium, and at least 1,500 others were "disappeared". Torture was systematic. From the first shot, Pinochet's junta attacked artists, musicians, folk singers, writers, and other cultural figures to drown opposition and dissent in blood. Renowned and beloved singer–songwriter Victor Jara was among the first killed. More than 40 bullets were found in his body.

Military sweeps throughout the capital inflicted intensifying violence on civilians and military units loyal to the President, culminating in a siege of the President's office in which Allende was killed.

Salvador Allende "7 dias ilustrados": Revista Argentina

Allende's physician and friend Dr José Quiroga was with the president when he died of his wounds. I met José at a conference on abolishing torture and assisting its survivors in 1983. Then many years later I worked with him while I was directing Survivors International in San Francisco and José, as he has for decades, was running the program he founded for torture survivors at the Venice Clinic in Los Angeles.

José is nearly always cheerful. In spite of the tragic and horrifying stories he hears as part of his work, in free moments he's relaxed, witty and full of fun. But once, when someone asked him about Allende, a cloud descended. His eyes grew grave and slowly filled with tears. When he could speak, José haltingly recited some of Allende's words from his final radio broadcast moments before the end: "I am certain that the seed we have planted in the good conscience of thousands and thousands of Chileans will not be shriveled forever … History is ours and people make history."

My life in Amnesty and the human rights movement is too long a story for these pages. Over more than 50 years since that first summer, I have performed diverse roles and tasks, and worked on many campaigns. A chronology of my involvement appears at the end of this book as Appendix 1. As reflected there, I have often been called upon to act as spokesperson. It was in that capacity, as western region director of Amnesty International USA, that I came to hear the voice of Carla Cristi.

Carla Cristi and the 77

For me, Carla Cristi's trembling voice, as much as the songs of Victor Jara, the poetry of Pablo Neruda or the stirring oratory of

José Zalaquett, is the voice of Chile under Fascist rule, suffering but indomitable. Scholars mostly contend now that Pinochet's junta did not meet all the defining criteria for Fascism. The distinctions may have merit, but I find the conclusion unpersuasive. Jackboots, summary executions, mass killings, "disappearances," systematic torture. Close enough.

Pinochet, like Hitler, wanted to enshrine myth as the only pure wellspring of culture. Independent art, especially Chile's socially conscious theater and film community, was to be swept away. Carla Cristi was one of 77 actors and theater workers given a deadline to leave the country or be killed. Some individually also endured repeated death threats, bomb scares, and assaults. Pinochet and his brown-shirts must have thought, with Heinrich Himmler, that, "What happens to these people can be the business of nobody else in the world."

Fortunately, they were wrong. Novelist Ariel Dorfman, who had barely escaped Chile with his life and freedom in 1973, was teaching at Duke in 1987, as he is today. Upon hearing of the threats, Ariel wrote an op-ed published in *The New York Times* on November 20, 1987. He began looking for an American movie star who'd bring attention to the situation. Meryl Streep was his first call, but she was filming in Australia, so Ariel called his friends Rose and Bill Styron.

Rose and William Styron and family at home, late 1980s.

Photo credit: Peter Simon, used by permission of Ronni Simon.

Rose had participated in an Amnesty fact-finding mission to Chile in 1974. She was a member of Amnesty USA's board of directors, and as an accomplished poet and activist, knew many people in the arts. The Styrons suggested Christopher Reeve. Ariel called Reeve at his home. Stunned to be asked, Chris Reeve later told reporters, "I said 'yes'. How do you say 'no' with 77 lives at stake? I mean, nothing else I was doing could possibly be that important."

The event he was to speak at in Santiago was summarily canceled by the junta, but organizers quickly moved the venue to a large garage where several thousand Chileans gathered to greet him. Before saying a word, his wave to the crowd, a simple gesture of friendship and solidarity, was met by a thunderous ovation. The experience left him awed and humbled. As he took the microphone the throng in unison sang their anthem, "He will fall." When the lights were suddenly shut off, all waited in silence for 30 minutes before listening to Reeve's brief message of concern for the 77. "That was unity such as I'd never seen," he said on his return.

Artists rise in solidarity

Ariel Dorfman contacted the Amnesty office in Los Angeles to see if we could keep the pressure from ebbing after Chris Reeve came home. Amnesty's press director, Judy Martinez, immediately reached out to activists in Hollywood for help. We devised a plan to hold a news conference at the LA Press Club, where we would assemble as many celebrities as possible to express their concern and solidarity. But we needed something powerful to bring the issue into vivid focus for the LA media.

Over a "Number 11" with double fries and a Coke at Hamburger Hamlet, Judy and I brainstormed, looking for a way to rivet the media and ensure that the threatened actors in Chile would know of our support and feel it. We decided to focus on one of the actors and try to speak with her by phone at the press conference. We chose Carla Cristi, who had just suffered a second death threat. I asked Nick Rizza to come down to LA from our office in San Francisco to translate.

Response to Judy's calls was strong. On extremely short notice, Malcolm McDowell, Mary Steenburgen, Ed Asner, Daryl Hannah, Hector Elizondo, and almost 50 other actors and directors took the stage with Amnesty International USA executive director Jack Healey. I summarized the situation described in our media advisory and then introduced Jack, who made a subdued, dignified statement.

Nick got Carla Cristi on the phone with a few fits and starts that had some reporters fidgeting. From her first words, her terror was palpable and heart-rending. Nick gave her our greetings and told her that not only were her colleagues watching, but through the LA media, the eyes and ears of our country were now on Chile. *"No estas solo, Señorita Cristi,"* Nick said finally. *"No estas solo."* He turned to translate for the English-language outlets. "You're not alone, I told her," he said, and started to translate her reply when a loud, furious male voice barked at us and at Carla over the phone line.

"¿Quién eres tú? Who are you?" Nick demanded to know in both languages. The man went on roaring curses and threats. Static made his shouting mostly indecipherable. Carla Cristi sobbed. For a moment, Nick waited in silence for her. Then, as we had arranged, Judy signaled to Hector Elizondo to come to the microphone.

The moment Carla heard Hector's voice, she buoyed. "Hector?" she asked incredulously. "Hector Elizondo?" They spoke quietly for a moment before the spy started barking again. At a signal from Nick, Hector said a few more kind words, promising to keep in touch. "You that's making all the racket?" Hector added calmly in Spanish, with Nick loosely translating. "You don't have to tell us who you are. We know."

Me speaking at Amnesty International USA's news conference on Pinochet's threats against Chilean artists, May 1988.

Photo credit: Mitzi Trumbo, used by permission of the photographer.

The man barked again. Looking around, I saw astonishment growing on the normally businesslike, world-weary faces of the reporters and camera operators. They may have believed us before. Now they felt it.

"It is everyone's business."

The work, as always, did not end there. Ariel didn't rest. Voices of the Chilean people's friends throughout the world became a sound Pinochet and his goons could not ignore. The Screen Actors Guild (SAG) and American Federation of Television and Radio Artists (AFTRA) issued statements of solidarity like the one sent by Actors' Equity. Calls poured into the State Department from California and New York Congressional offices.

From the time Christopher Reeve stepped off the plane in Santiago, threats against the 77 began to subside and none after that was ever carried out. One voice had become a chorus. Pinochet caved. He even made a lame attempt at saying the threats were little more than a prank at the expense of some incorrigibles in the Chilean theater, mocking his critics for falling for it. Nobody laughed.

Carla Cristi and her fellow artists were safe. Pinochet's credibility took a crushing blow from which he never recovered. Bit by bit, his façade of invincibility and the lethal tools he used to preserve his power fell away. After interning more than 80,000 and torturing tens of thousands of Chilean political prisoners over 15 years, a plebiscite in 1988 ousted Pinochet from the presidency, leading to the restoration of democracy. Pinochet hung onto a measure of power through the army for years but was nevertheless arrested in 2004 and eventually faced nearly 300 criminal charges. He died in 2006.

Why this memory? In nearly five decades of human rights campaigning, I have seen larger victories. I have had the honor of meeting many of those on whose behalf Amnesty and the movement struggle. But this one has always stayed close to my heart. I feel it when I listen to Violeta Parra's "Gracias a la Vida," when I hear Joan Baez sing "Oh Freedom," and in quiet moments of reflection with dear friends Judy Martinez and Rose Styron and with Bill Wipfler before he passed away. Like a star in the endless dark, our voices were raised together for the threatened artists of Chile and I will always believe we made a lifesaving difference that day for Carla and other faraway strangers living under tyranny's upraised boot.

Some scoff ruefully at the phrase "never again" uttered in the aftermath of the Holocaust and the Second World War, so battered and bedraggled is the oath after Idi Amin's Uganda, Pol Pot's Cambodia and countless other modern horrors. But that is to misunderstand the message. Neither the UN nor any treaty or alliance can always prevent atrocities, even those that descend into genocide. Never again means we will never again watch in silence and disbelief. For too long, Pinochet had acted with impunity. Not on that day, and never again after that. In the 1970s, Nixon, Kissinger, and the CIA had helped Pinochet take power and keep it, in the process abetting human rights violations against the Chilean people on a massive scale. But as the late 1980s witnessed the collapse of apartheid and the dismantling of the Berlin Wall, Pinochet's death threats against actors and artists were eventually revealed as the flailing of a dying monster.

In her speech to the Polish Senate on December 10, 1997, as the fiftieth anniversary year of the Universal Declaration of Human Rights began, Ginetta Sagan reminded her audience of Himmler's insistence that, "What happens to these people can be the business of nobody else in the world."

"To him and to all dictators, all torturers, with our eyes on the future we say, 'It is everyone's business.'" Taking a deep breath before reciting the words smuggled into her cell in a matchbox in 1945, she added, "And to prisoners of conscience huddling in dark prison cells anywhere on Earth, we say, "*Coraggio. Lavoriamo per te.*" (Courage, I am working for you.)

Some sounds never stop echoing. One of those for me is Carla Cristi's voice telling us how alone she had felt, jumping at every noise, cringing in her own home, in her own beloved city and country. In spite of her shivering, hers was a beautiful voice. By the time we said goodbye, I'd heard something new in it: hope.

In her career Carla was also a singer. I never heard her sing, but I know that today she is free to share happy moments with those she loves, to use her gifts, to think and speak as she believes. To live. Sing, Carla, wherever you are, and remember: You were not alone. You were not forgotten.

7
Koreatown: A dictator's long reach

> Democracy is the absolute value that makes for human dignity, as well as the only road to sustained economic development and social justice.
>
> —Kim Dae-jung (2004). *The 21st century and the Korean people: selected speeches of Kim Dae-jung, 1998–2004*

The power of place

One of the first things I remember learning as a boy just reaching the "age of reason" was the power of place to change and shape our lives. Our family had just moved to Palo Alto, California, from Estherville, Iowa. The profound contrast in atmosphere was my first experience of feeling like a stranger in my own country.

Sooner or later I have lived or worked in nearly every corner of the United States, an exposure I cherish as each has distinctive charms and marvels. New York's Saw Mill River Parkway in October; childhood summers in northwest Iowa; Giants games in Baghdad by the Bay; clam chowder at Lowell's in Seattle's magical Pike Place Public Market; deep-dish lunch at Gino's East in the Loop, the entire afternoon at the Art Institute, then dinner at The

Berghoff —do not skip the strudel; cherry blossoms, Da Vinci and the Hope Diamond in Washington, DC; all the unique roads and streets: Route 66, Beale Street, Frenchmen Street, Upper Grant, Olvera Street. What a ride in one nearly dead—or if not, I'd soon kill it—hand-me-down car after another!

Which brings me to Los Angeles in 1982, in an indestructible Dodge Dart, just hired as Amnesty USA's western region director and looking for a place to live. Amnesty board member Bill Watanabe, a prince, found us a huge, beautiful house on Roosevelt Avenue in a mostly Latino neighborhood between Koreatown and Interstate 10. The owners, 100-year-old Mr and 90-year-old Mrs House, rented us the gracious three-bedroom home five minutes from the Amnesty office for $700 a month. I thought I was dreaming. Thank you, Bill!

The neighborhood was, in many ways, as wonderful as the house, full of children, music, fireworks, and fun. Five-year-old Maria next door fell in love with our four-year-old Sean, and Jonny, at 13, was the heartthrob of the block, with quite a following of friends including some wild ones and a lively bevy of adorable admirers.

On the downside, there were two junkyard dogs often loose at night and a few sketchy characters up to no good. David and Jonny quickly established a reputation as nice boys who liked everybody but were definitely not the guys to get on the wrong side of. For Choppers, the brindle pit, and Jaws, the mongrel, during night walks, I carried a hammer in my belt. Just the sight of it jumping into my hand and my "Come ON!" sent them skidding and scurrying, so clearly they were not as dumb as they looked.

Over the next eight years, we moved three more times before leaving Los Angeles: first to Santa Monica, then Palmdale in the high desert, and finally to a small ranch in the San Gabriel Mountains. Each environment was profoundly different from the last, each rich in memories. But the moments I want to recall here began—and to some extent, were rooted—in our first LA home on the outskirts of Koreatown.

The surroundings at that time were culturally diverse, with a Russian Orthodox church, Greek shops, and a patchwork of predominantly Latino and some African American neighborhoods a few blocks out from Olympic Boulevard, the main artery of LA's Koreatown, from around La Brea to Vermont, paralleling the Mid-Wilshire District. Driving Olympic Boulevard, it was impossible not to recognize the size, power, and energy of the Korean community. I had been completely ignorant of this community, and I had no idea how deeply involved in its life I would become.

Becoming involved

It was inevitable, though. Human rights violations, including kidnappings, arbitrary imprisonment based on politically motivated prosecutions, unfair trials, and torture, had been systematic under South Korean dictators Park Chung-hee and Chun Doo-Hwan. As Amnesty's regional director, I continuously received from our Colorado office and publicized Urgent Action Appeals for South Korean prisoners of conscience.

Amnesty's press director Judy Martinez began regularly inviting the Korean *Street Journal* to our press conferences and sending them copies of our Urgent Action appeals. Then, as the 1988 Olympic Games in Seoul grew near, Amnesty mounted a campaign for a general amnesty for South Korea's nearly 400 prisoners of conscience.

My study of Korea's tragic history and complex politics deepened, made more and more personal by the people I saw every day in stores and on my way to work. When I felt sufficiently briefed, Judy arranged a visit to the *Street Journal*'s Koreatown offices so I could confirm our view that the outlet was fully independent, not a tool for a political party or faction.

As a test, I brought Publisher Joseph Cho a copy of Amnesty's report on conditions in North Korean prisons that was based on the experience of poet Ali Lameda. If Mr Cho had refused to accept the report from my hands or to discuss its contents, I would have suspected him of being beholden to Pyongyang. Instead, he took an interest and, in our conversation, revealed a fully independent view and a passion for democracy. As we parted, he told me, his voice heavy with emotion, that reunification "is every free Korean's dream, but might never be more."

Years later, Mr Cho was sued by Gene Kim, a power in the business community and a relative of South Korean dictator Chun Doo-Hwan, alleging he had used his newspaper to advance Communism and the interests of North Korea, and demanding $6 million for Gene Kim's own "community association". Testifying for Mr Cho, I was gratified when the test of independence I had administered proved sufficient to have the suit dismissed.

Diplomacy

When the Amnesty campaign got under way I asked for and was granted a meeting with the South Korean Consul General, where I laid out Amnesty's concerns and presented him with the names of some 388 political prisoners Amnesty regarded as prisoners of conscience. The official was polite and noncommittal, chiefly interested in making clear the strict limits on his mission and authority. Expecting that, I had come prepared. "I understand," I told him. "I appreciate that you would normally report the matter to Ambassador Kim Kyun-Won, whose latitude is naturally wider. However, in light of His Excellency's departure (Chun Doo-Hwan had just removed him after six years), should I now go through Ambassador Lilley, conveying your demurral?"

I had learned that James R. Lilley, a former CIA operative and Reagan appointee, was highly regarded in Seoul. I had absolutely no way of commanding Lilley's attention, but the Consul General didn't know that. His manner changed. For a moment, he measured me with a steely stare. At last, he picked up the Amnesty material from his desk, rose, and bowed slightly. After looking another moment into my eyes, he shook his head no, almost imperceptibly. "No?" I said at once. "Not necessary? So, my office will hear from you? Ah. *Gam-sa-ham-ni-da.*" ("Thank you.")

The campaign

In a strategy meeting, Judy Martinez and I brainstormed ways to inform the Korean community of our concerns. In addition to featuring a case on NPR's "Amnesty International Reports" program on KCRW in Santa Monica, Judy set up an interview with

Joseph Cho for a piece in the *Street Journal*. We wanted the campaign talked about before and during an upcoming Street Fair that annually attracted thousands of Korean Angelenos and others to Koreatown. We decided to produce T-shirts silkscreened with an image of the Korean peninsula and the names, in Korean and English, of 14 of the longest-held prisoners of conscience. We worked with young Amnesty activists in the Korean community to sell the shirts at the Street Fair. We also got a list of all US Olympic athletes going to Seoul and sent one T-shirt for each to the US Olympic Committee headquarters in Seoul. We expected the shipment to be interdicted, which it was, causing the stir we had hoped for.

At the Street Fair, a very drunk Gene Kim, visiting stalls and concessions as director of the Street Fair, lost his temper when he saw the T-shirts. Staggering and cursing, he eventually picked up a chair and assaulted a young student who was vending the shirts. Another student tried to stop him, and was also struck. Police were called in and Kim was detained, then released but profoundly, publicly embarrassed.

After my interview with Joseph Cho appeared, a Korean American who owned and operated the 76 station where I bought gas in Santa Monica took me aside and warned me to be careful. When the story broke about the melee at the Street Fair with Amnesty's T-shirts in the middle of it, he spoke to me again. Clearly thinking I wasn't taking his warning seriously, he told Tina, "Your husband should carry a gun now." It shook her, so I told her it was a little joke between him and me.

A dictator's long reach

That was in 1988, by which time I knew the risks of working in LA for human rights in Chun Doo-Hwan's South Korea. Five years earlier, in the spring of 1983, I had my first taste of it when, at the invitation of human rights activists in the Korean community who had read about my appointment as Amnesty's regional director in the Los Angeles Times, I appeared as Kim Dae-jung's opening speaker before a gathering of 5,000 Korean speaking Angelenos at the Greek Theater.

Kim Dae-jung (1924–2009), who received the 2000 Nobel Peace Prize, was sometimes called Korea's Mandela because he had endured repeated captivity for standing up to tyranny, first when he was kidnapped in Tokyo by the Korean Central Intelligence Agency (KCIA) under orders from Park Chung-hee. He was saved from assassination through a diplomatic intercession by US Ambassador Philip Habib. But after Chun Doo Hwan seized power, Kim Dae-jung was arrested and this time formally sentenced to death. After an intercession by Pope John Paul II for Mr Kim, a Catholic, his sentence was reduced to 20 years' imprisonment, and he was permitted exile.

The night before Mr Kim spoke at the Greek Theater, agents of the KCIA issued death threats against his retinue of bodyguards, warning them that if they appeared, their families in South Korea "could not be protected from reprisal". At Mr Kim's insistence, they stayed home. When I arrived, the event organizers told me they had received what they called a "credible" telephone warning that, "The stage will explode if Kim speaks tonight." It was made clear to me they would understand if I chose to speak briefly and then immediately leave or not appear at all under the circumstances. But they

clearly wanted me to stay. They didn't say why, but it seemed obvious to me they hoped that, as the only non-Korean in attendance,
my presence was very likely not in Seoul's calculation and might
act as a deterrent. I remember the moment so vividly, listening,
looking into their worried faces. I had no thought of leaving, but if
I had needed a clincher, while we were talking a troupe of Korean
American children scurried in and lined up in beautiful pale yellow
costumes for their dance number. I kept glancing at them, some
of them beaming, some jittering with excitement. Yeah, I thought,
I'm going to beat it and let these little kids take their chances. "It is
my honor to stay," I said quietly.

South Korean President Kim Dae-jung, January 5, 1998.

Photo credit: Public domain (Wikipedia Commons).

The speech, in Korean and without translation, lasted over four hours. But it was stirring throughout to watch as the expressions on thousands of people's faces responded to his words as one. There was no incident that night; my parting with Mr Kim was very warm, and I left with the same glow as everyone else who was there. The gentleman from the gas station was there, and he greeted me like family ever after. The sweet couple who owned the laundry that cleaned my shirts would never again accept any money from me.

A victory for human rights and democracy

Just after the 1988 Olympic Games concluded, the South Korean government announced a general amnesty, releasing 388 prisoners of conscience. I have no idea if the work we did in Los Angeles or even worldwide activism and agitation surrounding the Seoul Olympics played a role in bringing about the amnesty.

Mr Kim evidently thought so. In December 1988, Kim Dae-jung arranged for an award from the Korean Institute for Human Rights to Amnesty International USA "in recognition of your commitment, determination and unceasing effort to preserve the basic fundamental dignity of human rights in South Korea". Mr Kim was elected President of South Korea in 1998, succeeding Kim Young Sam, whose election had begun to restore South Korean democracy. Kim Dae-jung served until 2003, helping to stabilize and secure democratic institutions and fully restore human rights protections in law and practice.

When he passed away in 2009, I saw again all those tear-filled
eyes that moved and haunted me then and prompted this poem:

Kim Dae-jung in Los Angeles

Death didn't come for me
that death
which like a finger in the spine
can hint, pretend, or beckon
but wants steel and stench
and fire to break blood and bone
but last night
as I sat there at the Greek
waiting for bombs
a shot or a grenade thrown on the stage
I listened to a man whose every day
is lived without the promise
of tomorrow

They told me
Kim Dae-jung will speak tonight
to thousands gathered
in Los Angeles
They called him the Aquino of Korea
an honor if I could accept
the danger of his vanished retinue
no bodyguards tonight to search the crowd
    for killers
and to stand by him

Will I, American, speak first
sit by his side
and share this portion of his fate

they dare to hope my skin
my presence by itself
my nationality
may form a shield of flesh
as armed men, dogs and all the safeguards
practiced, trained, assured
have fled in fear

Korean children danced
made me ashamed to tremble
then as the great voice rang out
to the reverent throng
ten thousand dark eyes glistened

I understood the meaning
not the words
the hours passed
between the roar of laughter
and applause

So many cried to hear him
spin from recollection
out of bleak captivity
and timeless aspiration
a fabric of rough cloth but many colors
and those whose tears
had long since splashed
into a sea of loss
a sea of dread
are giant now with memories

The men who swore to kill him
slink away

guns pound against wet armpits
in a mockery of hearts
the weapons of the shameless face of Seoul
the bagmen and their kin
KCIA at home here in L.A

I see the living weep
and dream the dead
who yearned, but didn't live to see this day
I sit beside him while he tilts
like all before him armed with only words
against the mindless windmills
of a tyrant's deadly silence

—written at our home near Koreatown,
Los Angeles, the day after Kim Dae-jung's 1983 speech.

8
Buru Island: Indonesia's monstrous secret

I will not close my eyes, neither those in my head nor those in my soul, as the ship carries me away, along with my future, my dreams, and my beliefs. Buru Island is no happy land somewhere; it's but a way station on my journey in life—though to believe even that much will require no small measure of hope.

—Pramoedya Ananta Toer, (1988). *The Mute's Soliloquy*

Crossroads: a point at which a crucial decision must be made that will have far-reaching consequences. —
Oxford English Dictionary

Pramoedya Ananta Toer.

Photographer unknown; cf. Jassin, H.B. 1955.

An anniversary almost nobody knows

On September 22, 1989, ten years to the day from the liberation and return home of the last political prisoners to leave the penal colony on Indonesia's Buru Island, I stayed late at the Amnesty office in LA, not ready to leave memories that had suddenly seized me. Alone in the now dimly lit office, I watched traffic swimming by on Sixth Street and to the southwest Wilshire Boulevard. It was almost nine but still rush hour by the look of it. The stream of tail lights hypnotized me. I rested my forehead against the window pane and let it all come back in a red river of memories. The horror imposed on so many human beings in a faraway country by a dictator abetted in mass murder by the US and ignored by most of the world; the apparent hopelessness of the fate of tens of thousands of untried political prisoners and the futility, for almost a decade, of international intercessions. And the campaign to free them that I believe became a thread in the skein of causality that led to that day, a decade gone, of freedom, fluttering banners, and tearful reunions. It was the most important and effective human rights work I had ever been part of, and one of the best kept secrets in modern history.

In the years since Buru Island's 14,000 political prisoners were freed in a general amnesty along with more than 20,000 others held for a decade in other concentration camps throughout the archipelago, I had been involved in many campaigns, had served as board chairperson of Amnesty USA and chairperson of the International Council Meeting, and for seven years had been western region director. So, with the passage of time and so many intervening challenges, the Indonesia campaign of 1976–1977 had mostly faded from memory.

That evening, as brake lights flickered and car horns quarreled, the memories returned. Two hours earlier, noticing the circled date on my office calendar while flicking off the light to head home, I froze, stunned, and had to return to my desk and sit down. I wanted to call and share the moment with David Hawk, Larry Cox, or Bill Frelick, who had worked on the campaign, or Ginetta and Leonard Sagan, Scott Harrison and Ellen Moore, Whitney Ellsworth, Rose Styron, Barbara Sproul, or Bill Wipfler, Amnesty colleagues and friends I knew would remember the work and fully appreciate the significance of the anniversary. But the Sagans were out of the country and all the rest lived in other time zones; it was already too late.

I wondered who else, sitting at home or in offices around the world, had marked the anniversary. I was thinking of Leonore Ryan, Indonesia coordinator for Amnesty Australia, who had passed away. After corresponding about cases for two years, Leonore and I met in Gotemba, Japan, in 1976 at an Amnesty development conference. Her letters, brief and incisive, did not prepare me for meeting her. In her sixties at least, she had a mischievous twinkle in her merry blue eyes. Tough, wry, roguish, and more than a little salty, she kept me laughing at an otherwise quite dignified gathering.

I was thinking, too, of colleagues in Dutch, German, UK, and Japanese sections who had worked on the Indonesia campaign in the 1970s. Had what we had done together been lost to time in just a decade? Or were some of them, like me, remembering

on this night? So I sat at my desk and wrote a poem. I don't
know how, but it helped me contain the inundating memories.
Here it is:

On Buru Island
Carrion can sleep peaceful now
on Buru Island
no more *tapols* scavenging
for bloated cows
or cats or rats
after a day of making the *kodim* richer
They used to come
gaunt reeds
too slim for wind to mire
sniffing for cuisine morte by moonlight
while Pramoedya spun a fable
so the guards would listen in
insinuating dreams of home
to haunt the soldiers
watching him

The *tapols* are free in Java now
in Kalimantan, Dili and Baucau
no PKI jokes told in Jogja anymore
no upstart protests in Bandung
and the coughing has stopped
on Buru Island

All coughing, sobbing, snoring
groaning, choking
murmur of dreams
tenacity of wheezing lungs

> or heartbeats drumming
> fourteen thousand times
> each second
> an S.O.S from zombie land
> a thrum that, vanishing
> has made a god of silence
> on Buru Island

To make the poem less inscrutable for family and friends, I later added an explanatory note about place names and Indonesian language references like *tapols*, short for *tahanan politik*—political prisoners, and *kodim*—the military commander of a region or camp where forced labor was performed.

But what could a few words say, in any language? Tens of thousands of political prisoners suffering inhuman conditions for over a decade. Hundreds of thousands killed in the coup of 1966—university students, laborers, members of the Indonesian Communist Party (PKI), and other leftist organizations, and in a racist pogrom, perhaps 200,000 or more ethnic Chinese Indonesians, by Suharto's troops. Systematic torture throughout a vast system of prisons and camps.

Pramoedya Ananta Toer

Too many souls, too much suffering and injustice to take in. That is why I wanted my poem to include at least one of Buru's prisoners by name. I chose Pramoedya Ananta Toer for many reasons, of which the most personal was a letter I received from one of his daughters a few months after his liberation. She wrote on very thin paper in a tiny, delicate hand, addressing the letter to "our dear friends Amnesty International".

The letter, three pages long on both sides, detailed a litany of restrictions her father was enduring, intolerable impositions similar to a banning order in apartheid South Africa. I confess I was emotionally worn out by the time I got to the letter's last paragraph, but her closing was a draught of pure refreshment to my soul: "I don't write to trouble you with these problems, but to honor you with the truth. And to say from my heart thank you. Papa is home."

Writing about it helped, but just the same, I felt a strange sense of isolation. Of knowing a story that would never be told.

Huang Wen-Hsien and the centrality of research

Most of all in that moment, I wondered about Huang Wen-Hsien. Huang served as Amnesty's researcher on Indonesia and the Philippines beginning in 1974 and by 1977 became Head of Region. At that time, Amnesty's research complement at its Secretariat in London was no more than 50 or 60, covering among them, to the extent possible, the entire world. All the prisoner dossiers distributed to local chapters in 45 countries came from those few desks.

Even if they had today's technology and communications capabilities, their task would have been impossible. For me, it is all the more remarkable, therefore, that researchers like Huang Wen-Hsien were able to generate an impressive volume of painstakingly vetted reports that stood up to close scrutiny and created such a vexing challenge for human rights violating regimes accustomed to acting with impunity.

When the Nobel Committee awarded Amnesty International the Peace Prize in 1977, it cited the quality and rigor of Amnesty's research, as well as the discipline the organization exercised by giving governments the opportunity to respond to allegations in writing before reports were published. The Committee also praised strict avoidance of personalization or sensationalism as hallmarks of its credibility.

The standard for human rights research and intercession had been, and in some respects still is, the International Committee of the Red Cross (ICRC). The ICRC's unparalleled access to prisons and other sites of large-scale human rights abuses arose in part from its practice of filing its reports only to the government in question and studious avoidance of inflammatory or intemperate language in its representations.

Huang Wen-Hsien in 1975.

Photo credit: family photo used by permission of the family.

Other organizations, like the International League for Human Rights and the International Commission of Jurists, had for years filed public reports, largely for experts and policymakers to consider if they wished. Amnesty's signal contribution to the human rights movement was to be the first NGO to use the information in its reports and dossiers to organize a global network of volunteers to speak out, write letters and telegrams, communicate with third-party governments and other levers of influence, and mount pressure on offending regimes for specific human rights objectives. Pressure, from the time Amnesty was founded by Peter Benenson, Seán MacBride, and others in 1961, primarily for unconditional release of named individuals considered "prisoners of conscience," which Amnesty defined as those "imprisoned or otherwise physically restricted for their beliefs, their race, ethnic origin, language, or religion who have not used or advocated violence". Today, Amnesty International produces reports and conducts human rights campaigning on issues across the entire spectrum of human rights. But in the 1970s, the mandate was narrowly drawn in hopes of giving what was still a fledgling movement a chance to succeed.

In 1973 and 1974, when I first volunteered for Amnesty, I worked with Joan Baez, Ginetta Sagan, former United Farm Workers organizer Kit Bricca, and others to establish new chapters all over California. There were almost 50 by the time others took over the work. Many of these chapters were among Amnesty USA's most active local groups for decades, and over 50 years later, some of them are still at it. My niece Monica joined Group 19 in Palo Alto more than 30 years after I worked with them on their first cases: prisoners of conscience in the USSR, Iran, and Indonesia. My own chapter was assigned case dossiers for Aleksandr Feldman, a *refusenik*—a person, often a dissident, denied permission to emigrate by the Soviet Union—who was imprisoned in Belozerski, USSR, and Ismail Bakri, a member of the PKI. Bakri had been sentenced to life imprisonment in Java for his role in a legal political party that Suharto and his New Order regime retroactively outlawed when he seized power in 1966. We celebrated when Aleksandr was released from Cherskonskaya Prison and permitted to emigrate. But in the life of our chapter, we got nowhere on behalf of Ismail Bakri.

How Indonesia became the focus of my work with Amnesty in the 1970s

Because I was sometimes called on to coach some of the groups we had formed, I learned that nearly all of them had been assigned Indonesian cases, and every experience was the same. The Suharto regime ignored all requests for information. Members of Congress were also unresponsive. Few had ever heard of Amnesty International—the Nobel Peace Prize was almost four years in the future. Some thought the organization had something to do with pardoning draft resisters. Allegations of torture were met with silence or skepticism.

I was pretty much resigned to failure on the Indonesia front until I met Dirk Boerner at an Amnesty gathering in Palo Alto, California. Dirk was a member of Amnesty West Germany whose outdoor equipment business periodically brought him to the US. He told a series of vignettes about the ingenious and determined work done by Amnesty groups in Europe and about former prisoners who attributed their freedom "to you, who do not forget us".

After his speech, I spoke with Dirk about the large number of assigned cases from Indonesia and the persistent futility of our intercessions. He confirmed it was the same in Amnesty West Germany. Dirk told me about a system developed in the Dutch and German sections called country coordination. Coordination groups had been formed there, comprised of country experts and Amnesty activists who accepted responsibility for advising local chapters on how best to put pressure on the government in question.

One of the first set up in the Netherlands was the Indonesia Coordination Group. I got contact information from Dirk, one of the most knowledgeable, well-organized, and conscientious Amnesty leaders I ever met. Just before we parted, Dirk had a second thought. He touched my shoulder as I turned to go. "But David," he said, looking into my eyes, "don't take this on unless you're prepared to put a great deal of time and effort into it. It would be better not to try than to raise expectations that can't be met."

"Just what I was thinking," I told him. "Dirk, I'm not an expert on any country, not even my own." He laughed. "Knowing that is a good place to start," he said. "For something so important, it should be possible to find people who can help you. But if not, it is probably best for you to back away." Good advice, I reflected.

Yet the words "back away" kept echoing. Words a person with Irish blood in their veins—or at least this son of an Irish mother—cannot hear as anything but a challenge. If I can find somebody qualified, I thought, great. But I guess I already knew. Thoughts of Ismail Bakri, Pramoedya Ananta Toer, Bud Budiardjo, and others whose cases I had learned about and worked on to no avail had me by the back of the neck.

My wife Tina joined me as I headed for the car. "What's wrong?" she asked, looking a little alarmed.

"I don't know," I admitted. "Something Dirk just said, I guess."

"What? He's so nice!"

"You know we've been talking in the group about Indonesia. He told me about a way to organize it better, but he said if I can't put a ton of time and work into it, to back away."

"Are you thinking about it?" she wondered.

"Back away?"

"Are you, though?"

I didn't know how to answer. We drove home in silence, not unusual because a mile from the conference site she was fast asleep, as she often is on long car rides. When we got home, she woke up asking, "What? What did you say, David?"

"Nothing, baby."

"Oh, I thought you said, 'That'll be the day.'" That got a laugh out of me. I realized I had been grinding my teeth all the way home. "You're right," I told her. "That's exactly what I said."

Crossroads

That's the way I have always experienced crossroads. By the time you're standing there, it's already too late to turn back.

So I reached out to the Dutch, German, and British Indonesia country coordinators, who encouraged me. The UK coordinator, also a non-expert, sent me a bibliography of required reading she had been given that would choke a horse, even an Irish one. I waded into it over the next few months. In the summer and fall of 1974, I cobbled together a list of ideas passed on to me by my European counterparts and sent them to Leonore Ryan, whom I had just met by mail, in Melbourne, Australia. She was thrilled with what she called an "overdue transfusion for Amnesty Australia's tired blood".

Leonore asked me if I had corresponded with Huang Wen-Hsien after he approved me as coordinator. Yes, I had told him about Bill Frelick, a brilliant young activist from Oberlin who had taken the initiative to inform US corporations with holdings and joint ventures in Indonesia about the high number of prisoner-of-conscience cases there and evidence of the systematic use of torture. "Now you're talking," Leonore said in her next letter. "Good on Bill. Those murderers aren't going to stop unless they have to. All the letters in the world won't do it. But a call from big oil, or one of those satellite companies? And what about the World Bank?"

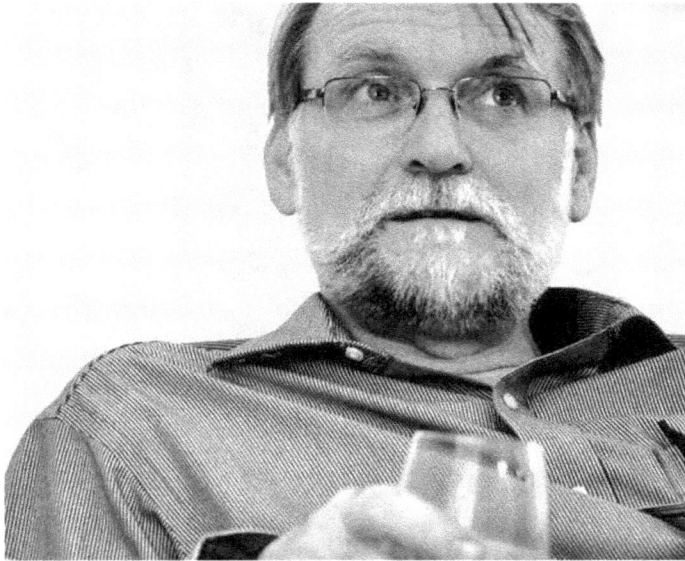

Bill Frelick, now Director of the Refugee and Migrant Rights Division of Human Rights Watch, in conversation at a conference in Brussels.

Photographer unknown, used by permission of Bill Frelick.

That's how it went and that's how it always goes. Nothing starts with you; nothing gets done without help. One idea leads to another. Most do not work, but some succeed, and those create new possibilities that wouldn't have existed otherwise.

So we were campaigning for the long-term prisoners even before there was a formally declared Amnesty International campaign. But it was far too little, even taken together, either to move the stone wall in Jakarta or to engage a deeply vested US government on behalf of the *tapols*.

Along the way, the stories, the photos, and the cruel force of vicarious sorrow sank into me. The faces of prisoners and their grieving families still haunt me at times today, the way they did then. Less and less frequently as time goes on, but I'm never completely free of their stricken faces, those we were already too late to help and those who languished and died while we kept knocking on doors that would not open.

I can only recover from such sad thoughts by imagining the docks in Java as the last freed Buru Island prisoners, Pramoedya among them, emerge, square their emaciated shoulders, walk with heads held high down the gangplank and get the first glimpses of their loved ones.

Why we choose this work

That moment, multiplied thousands of times, is the reason I am writing this chapter. I want those who may remember me to know what made me choose the work I did. For all of us in the movement, I think, just to play a part in bringing about such a day—the beaming smiles, hugs, kisses, and tears—and even more all the ordinary little pleasures that would follow in their lives from that day down to this—motivated our work as much as the suffering and injustice that fired our outrage or the courage and resolve with which so many grappled with tyranny before and after they were jailed and tortured.

When my family gets together for a big meal, a birthday cake, and a game or two around a long table, I sometimes think of them, grandparents now like Tina and me, gathering at home or in a restaurant banquet room, telling stories all but their youngest have heard, teasing the little ones, laughing and sharing a meal in cherished company. Out of the charnel house, in the bosom of their loved ones.

So here, as well as I can remember it, is what we did.

What we did

Amnesty International campaigned from early in 1976 through December of 1977, when Jakarta declared a general amnesty and the releases began. That is all of it in one sentence, but for a long time, it looked like it would never happen.

Huang Wen-Hsien, just appointed and getting the lay of the land in the research department, did not answer my first few letters in 1974 about the lack of progress on Indonesian cases. I learned later that before he had sufficient time or information to reply, Huang was already urging Amnesty's head of research to commission a full report on Indonesia as the basis for a concerted campaign. In his disciplined way, Huang did not share with me or other coordinators, as far as I knew, any part of the discussion at the Secretariat. He only told me, in response to a letter in which I expressed mounting frustration, that a report on long-term imprisonment was under consideration. "Please be patient, David," Huang wrote. "I'm doing my best."

The following year, Huang and fellow researcher Tom Jones completed a report on human rights violations in the Philippines. I read it in Gotemba, Japan, just before it was released and was greatly inspired and encouraged by it. It was one of the most thoroughly documented, hard-hitting yet measured reports I had seen from the organization up to then, or ever since.

The Philippines report was under media embargo for some time while the Marcos regime was given an opportunity to respond to its allegations of systematic torture and imprisonment of government critics, labor leaders and other perceived enemies of the dictatorship, so Huang was able to concentrate on Indonesia. It may have been just chance that this opportunity arrived when it did. But whether by instinct or intellection, early in 1976, Huang recognized a moment in which what had never been possible to move might just be moved after all.

What changed

Eventually I learned what some, perhaps most of the developments were that must have been part of Huang's calculation, including these four:

First, Huang learned that an Indonesian former general and diplomat named Benni Moerdani was rising in power and influence—he eventually became Vice President. His rise was significant because after being posted to Seoul, he returned to Jakarta convinced that South Korea's large population of political prisoners was a liability to them in bilateral relations with Japan, Australia, and the US. Prof. Benedict Anderson of Cornell's Modern Indonesia Project, who had reliable sources in Indonesia, confirmed Moerdani's views and his appeals to Suharto.

Second, Huang's own sources inside Indonesia had identified major discrepancies between the number of *tapols* the regime acknowledged holding at a prison in Java versus the much larger number they knew to be held there. Two of Indonesia's very few lawyers who represented *tapols*, Yap Thiam Hien and Adnan Buyung Nasution, were both in Gotemba for Amnesty's Pan-Pacific Development Conference of June 1976. The three of us met over Suntory for Adnan, Sapporo for me, and tea for

Yap. At a barbecue the afternoon before and again that evening, Yap seemed to grow about as inebriated as the company he was in while drinking only tea. He had an unforgettable silent laugh that he wasn't stingy with.

Before the story swapping started, Yap talked about the numbers in Java and suggested there could be similar discrepancies throughout the system. In their communications with Huang, they told me they had also addressed the inherent limitations and pitfalls of work for individual prisoners. Nasution stressed that Amnesty had fallen into Jakarta's trap by developing dossiers on the relatively few cases where information was available. Almost all were PKI cases, a fact regime fixer Lim Bian Kee used to paint Amnesty as a Communist sympathizer in his talks with Congressional staff in Washington and during the junkets he arranged for them in Bali. The way out of the trap, Yap and Nasution argued, was to campaign for a general amnesty.

Third, an internal policy document called *Bapreru*, prepared by Indonesian intelligence, had been uncovered by his sources and leaked to Huang. The document called for relocating the families of all remaining Category B prisoners—those considered enemies of the New Order but against whom no evidence of criminal wrongdoing could be brought—to the prison camps holding their loved ones. Relocation of women and children to concentration camps where prisoners performed forced labor on near-starvation rations would have amounted to the regime's "Final Solution" to the *tapol* problem: slow extermination in internal exile.

Finally, Huang was aware that in the United States, new legislation sponsored by Congressman Don Fraser had been passed. The new law required the State Department to report to Congress yearly on the human rights performance of all countries with US relations, whether friendly or adversarial. Prior to the so-called 502B reports, no binding mechanism existed for assessing US military, security, and police transfers in relation to abuses of human rights in recipient countries. That linkage meant that Indonesia could lose millions of US dollars each year if the regime was found to be guilty of human rights abuses on a large scale or if improvements in their record could not be demonstrated.

Indonesia had up to then succeeded in sanitizing its image with active cooperation from one US administration after another. Because the CIA had been deeply involved in bringing Suharto to power, many in the career foreign relations bureaucracy, especially during the Nixon and Ford administrations, were eager to foster an image of the New Order government as a Southeast Asian bastion against Communism. When Indonesia invaded the newly freed former Portuguese colony of East Timor in 1975, the US deemed it an "annexation," while the East Timorese resistance movement, known as *Fretilin,* fought on, and much of the rest of the world called for Timorese self-determination in a series of UN resolutions.

Also in 1975, the war in Vietnam had just ended. Images of people trying to flee in helicopters cast a final net of shame over a disgraceful chapter in American imperialist history.

The Khmer Rouge of Cambodia seized the moment to engage in a horrific ideological war that took almost two million lives, called by some an "autogenocide".

Having had so much to do with the tragedies and horrors unfolding in Southeast Asia, the US government then decided to look the other way. Many of us hoped US scrutiny of Indonesia's record would intensify when President Jimmy Carter was elected. It did not. Perhaps it was because Carter, who had proclaimed human rights "the soul of US foreign policy", so feared the rise of militant Islam as a political force that he chose to embrace the Shah of Iran and ignore all calls for bilateral intercession on behalf of the *tapols* in Suharto's Indonesia. I don't know if that was the reason. But the record does not lie. I greatly admire President Carter's many historic contributions to human rights, but he did nothing to help free the *tapols* and was largely silent about the murderous occupation of East Timor as well.

Amnesty's first ever country campaign

One more factor played an important part in what was to follow for Amnesty's work for human rights in Indonesia. Early in 1976, faced with a growing number of deaths under torture in Uruguay, Amnesty launched its first ever country campaign. Amnesty sections around the globe bombarded Montevideo with letters, telegrams, and telexes from ordinary people and the experts and other notable activists they were able to mobilize. Still, the conditions in Uruguayan prisons remained largely unchanged until Amnesty brought the campaign to Washington.

David Hawk.

Photographer unknown, used by permission of David Hawk.

With leadership from Amnesty USA board member Bill Wipfler, director of the Latin America desk at the National Council of Churches, Rick Wright, director of the Washington office, and Amnesty USA executive director David Hawk—a seasoned campaigner who in the 1960s co-led the anti-war Moratorium and, before that, participated in tough civil rights work in the South under the banner of the Student Nonviolent Coordinating Committee (SNCC)—Amnesty persuaded a Congressional committee to hold hearings on AI's Uruguay report. Change in Uruguay followed swiftly as a direct response by the regime to the prospect of losing military aid over the deaths under torture it had tried to cover up. The remarkable impact of the Uruguay campaign convinced some in the International Secretariat hierarchy that country campaigning had promise. Huang's lobbying for a campaign on behalf of the *tapols* finally found receptive ears. Huang filed a brief report summarizing the conditions on Buru Island and attaching to it a précis of the *Bapreru* document.

The Buru Island mini-campaign

I had been elected to the Amnesty USA board in December 1975. That position allowed me to get funds allotted to underwrite the costs of what was called the "Buru Island mini-campaign" of 1976. I used some of the money to take Huang's Buru report to editorial boards such as the *Chicago Tribune*, *Detroit Free Press*, *St. Louis Post-Dispatch*, *Portland Oregonian*, *San Francisco Chronicle*, and *Seattle Times*, newspapers of record in cities represented by members of key Congressional committees.

I spoke to Amnesty gatherings at the University of Chicago, Stanford, UC Santa Cruz, the University of Washington, and the University of Southern California (USC). I hosted gatherings for guest speaker Carmel Budiardjo of the UK's TAPOL organization, which she founded and directed. Carmel's husband, Bud, was in prison for his role in the PKI.

Interest in the report everywhere I went varied from none at all to some shock, in particular on the part of editorial writers at the Chicago Tribune, that none of this had come to light before. Bob Landauer, distinguished editorial page editor for the Oregonian, called it "a very well-kept secret, if it's true".

At Huang's suggestion, I drafted an "open letter" about the *tapols* that Carl Rogers, co-founder of Vietnam Veterans Against the War, who was brought on to help me with press coverage, pitched to the outlets I had visited and strategic others. Carl used a clipping service to track appearances of the letter. They were few. Some excerpted parts as a letter to the editor. Nobody ran the whole thing, but it got out there enough that years later, a State Department official burst into the meeting room during a lunch meeting David Hawk and I were having with dear old Charlie Runyon about ratification of the UN Human Rights Covenants and loudly declared that my letter had disrupted State's "quiet diplomacy" and had probably cost many lives, before storming out after I failed to respond. Charlie smiled at me. "Somebody has taught you not to take the bait," he mused. "My mother," I told him. "No arguing once the food is on the table."

Carl organized a news conference at the UN Church Center with me as presenter and David Hawk to backstop me on general Amnesty questions. We waited a long time for reporters from a dozen invited outlets, including some that had told Carl to expect them, but the only ones to show up were the Harvard *Crimson* and the Voice of America (VOA). Carl set up a phone interview with Nat Hentoff at the Village Voice after VOA and the *Crimson* left. Hentoff was interested and eventually outraged, especially about the *Bapreru* plan, and wrote a piece. He was the first person I heard call it a "Final Solution". But there was no avoiding the impression, that day at the UN Church Center and pretty much throughout the Buru Island mini-campaign, that we were failing.

Me speaking at a demonstration outside the Indonesian Consulate in San Francisco, April 15, 1975.

Photographer unknown, photo owned by me.

Timing: The impact of the Nobel Peace Prize

Timing, they say, is everything. In October of 1977, one year almost to the day after that disappointing news conference, Larry Cox, Amnesty USA's newly appointed press director, booked the UN Church Center again to release Huang Wen-Hsien's book-length report titled *Long Term Imprisonment in Indonesia.* Huang was the speaker, with David Hawk, Larry, and me there to take AIUSA questions. Looking out at a jostling crowd of reporters with microphones and television cameras labeled CBS, ABC, and NBC, I marveled silently at how things change. But the reason for Amnesty's sudden media appeal was no mystery: a week before, the Nobel Committee had announced the awarding of its 1977 Peace Prize to Amnesty International, recognizing by so doing the importance of promoting and protecting human rights for the cause of peace in the world.

News stories arising from the press conference and subsequent interviews prominently featured the Indonesia campaign and the Congressional hearings that David Hawk and Rick Wright had arranged with a Congressional committee. The hearing put the matter of Indonesia's human rights record squarely into the 502B process.

I believe it was the combined effect of potential implications arising from the Congressional hearing and coverage of Huang's blistering report in the media that rocked Jakarta and cracked its formerly impenetrable wall of silence. This, I also believe, was what Huang had visualized as much as three years earlier.

I still think of Huang as I first saw him, deep in thought at his desk in a cramped office at the Secretariat, then in Covent Garden. I arrived with Tina during our second honeymoon just a few weeks before Huang's report was due to be released. Staff aides were working late. The report was unfinished and time was running short. Huang's highly skilled, tireless executive assistant, Isobelle Jaques, a dedicated and irreplaceable information manager and communicator, shooed everybody away, whispering to me, "He's thinking."

"C'mon," Tina whispered, and we left. I remember Huang's total fixity. He held a few fingers to his temple as if taking a call on an invisible phone. Isobelle was right. Do not disturb.

Huang's gambit

Huang met his deadline. I stayed late a couple of nights that week to help. During those hours, we went from being valued colleagues to being friends. And before I left him, near midnight, as I was hurrying to get my stuff and get out before they locked the place for the night, he stopped me with a look and said something I will never forget: "To make this matter to Jakarta, the report must do something they don't expect. Something they're certain we wouldn't do."

I had no idea what he had in mind or why he said "do" and not "allege". None of us knew the Nobel Prize was coming in just days. Huang was evidently sure the contents of the report in and of themselves had to be sufficiently upsetting to Jakarta that they would react. "OK," I said, waiting.

"We—you—may be accused of exaggeration, or worse," he said, looking evenly at me.

"They've been saying we're Communists for years, Huang,"

"You must be prepared for this to be different," he said quietly.

I had read the draft but had paid little attention to the section on his research methodology. It was there that Huang's historic gambit was hiding in plain sight. Huang had taken the discrepancy in numbers of *tapols* held in Java's main prison that had been documented by Yap and Nasution and extrapolated it across the entire prison system. By doing so, Huang was making the vital points that neither Indonesia's silence nor its dismissal of criticism could be trusted and that, in the absence of verifiable information shared by the regime, Amnesty had no choice but to challenge Jakarta's version. The report's thrust was summarized in this sentence: "Amnesty International estimates that there are at least 55,000 untried political prisoners in Indonesia, and perhaps as many as 100,000."

The actual number of Category B prisoners still held in 1977 was approximately 35,000. Whether Huang believed the true number was higher or simply used a methodological device to gall Jakarta into breaking their silence is a question I never asked him. If indeed, as I suspect, he knew the higher number could be an exaggeration and expected Suharto, Ashari, and even Lim Bian Kee to take the bait, he had read them perfectly.

It may be useful to note here that Huang Wen-Hsien, like his principal adversary, the cunning spy and fixer Lim Bian Kee, was a chess master. Huang may have turned over many times in his mind the question, "Will Lim see through this?" Huang was dangling, in effect, Amnesty's queen—the organization's hard-earned reputation for understatement and rigor—in hopes it would be too tantalizing a target for Lim and his counterparts in Tokyo, Canberra, Amsterdam, Bonn and London to resist attacking with the facts on their side.

Ironically, crucially, with the Nobel announcement, Huang's bold gambit was offered at what would suddenly become the apex moment of Amnesty's global acclaim and credibility. On October 18, arriving at the Congressional Subcommittee hearing on Capitol Hill, I had a front-row seat on history unfolding even before the testimony began. Ambassador Ashari paced in an anteroom outside the hearing chamber, having been asked for but unwilling to present his credentials. I stood at a slight distance and listened. He spoke in Indonesian to an aide who was going in. I have no idea what was said, but his fidgeting spoke volumes. Before Ashari left, we made eye contact. I guess I was enjoying his obvious agitation, and maybe noticing it, he glared at me. Anonymously, though. He clearly had no idea who I was. I don't know why exactly, but that put a smile on my face so stubborn I had to suppress it with some difficulty before going in. Absolutely nothing in public life ever pleased or comforted me more than anonymity. That's my Grandma Bowen living on in me, I guess.

I had to fight down laughter when, in the midst of testimony, Ashari's aide's tape recorder loudly clicked as the tape ran out. He fumbled with it in his lap, dropped it, ducked under the table, and finally came up with a sheepish grin. As Ashari must have instructed, the aide protested, and the State Department witness chimed in that Amnesty's numbers were hugely exaggerated. The aide contended Amnesty was being manipulated by "Communists like Carmel Budiardjo" in a clear attempt to smear an important US ally and stalwart foe of Communism.

"How many prisoners are held, in fact?" a Committee member asked.

Snap! The trap was sprung. In declaring that Jakarta was holding *only* 35,000 political prisoners without trial ten years after their arrest, the Embassy broke the stone wall of silence behind which the regime had carried out its murderous work since the coup of 1966. If Ashari thought the discrediting correction would be met by censure for Amnesty, the briefing he got that afternoon from his aide and the subsequent publication of the hearing testimony in the Congressional Record must have hit him like a jab in the eye followed, while that still hurt, by a sledgehammer to the chest.

The tenor of Congressional reaction was something like this: "Only 35,000? Is that what you said? Untried, uncharged, for how many years?"

Huang had protected Amnesty from censure by declaring and documenting that its numbers were an estimate based on known discrepancies and silence from Jakarta. Still, maybe if it had ended there, Lim and his counterparts might have bribed and flattered their way out of it. But then came the Nobel and the media coverage of it, with Indonesia in every other line. There, in black and white, to be read by CEOs, third-party embassies, and members of Congress over breakfast, was not only Amnesty's newfound standing but also its allegations against the Suharto regime and, perhaps most distressingly for the high command, their Embassy's self-incriminating protestations. That, for me, was incontrovertible proof that Huang Wen-Hsien had understood his opponent, who ultimately failed to understand him. On our last evening together in London, Huang had told me, "Indonesia is a shame culture. To understand it, you must watch Javanese shadow puppetry, in which good and evil keep changing places. Jakarta will not respond to what others say is wrong. In a shame culture, perception, perspective, is everything. They won't be cowed by censure. They'll reject or ignore it. But if they can be made to falter, to blunder, that, I think, could be the door in the wall. To rid themselves of the shame such a blunder would heap upon them—to save face—they might do almost anything. Even let the *tapols* go."

The *tapols* come home

These calculations proved their value only a few months later. One day after my 31st birthday, on November 30, 1977, Indonesia announced a general amnesty. The first releases were carried out in January 1978. It was more than another year before Pramoedya and about 150 others who had refused to recant their beliefs were finally removed from Buru Island and brought home to Java by ship. "I will not recant beliefs I have never held," Pramoedya said simply. It cost him more months in that godforsaken corner of hell, but he went home with his honor.

I never saw Huang Wen-Hsien after he left the Secretariat, so we never got to conduct a post mortem on our work together. David Hawk ran into Huang while David was directing the Cambodia Documentation Commission and Huang was working for the

UN High Commissioner for Refugees (UNHCR). They had dinner together at a restaurant in Aranyaprathet near the Thai Cambodia border and I suppose had something like the talk Huang and I never got to share. David remembers that Huang praised the Amnesty USA campaign, deflecting credit for his initiative and brilliance that were due from history.

In 2015, not long after Huang Wen-Hsien passed away, his sons Han and Kiat asked me to share my memories of their late father. We recorded a couple of hours of recollections. I was delighted to meet Huang's sons in that way. What I did not expect was that revisiting those memories would be a great catharsis for me. For a week afterwards, in recurring reveries, I was visited by ghosts of old friends and colleagues who had passed away: Ginetta Sagan, who brought me into the work; Dirk Boerner, who challenged me; Leonore Ryan, who made me laugh; and of course Huang Wen-Hsien. Yap Thiam Hien, with whom I had spent such illuminating and memorable hours in Japan, also joined the spectral gathering.

Five years have passed since those interviews with Han and Kiat Wen-Hsien. Then, in 2020, I heard from Ellen Moore that there might be interest in the recordings at Columbia University's Center for Human Rights Documentation and Research, which houses Amnesty USA's archives from its now over 60-year history. So I reached out to Han and, through him, Kiat to ask permission in case Columbia wants them. It was so good to be back in touch. When I read Han's messages, I remembered his voice. When I first heard Han's voice on the phone, I heard Huang too. The brothers sent me the photos seen here. My favorite is the one taken by his fellow researcher, Tom Jones, of Huang in the Bighorn Crags Wilderness, smiling. It made me remember his smile that seemed always to come from deep within. Thank you, Han and Kiat. Thanks, Tom.

Huang Wen-Hsien in the Bighorn Crags Wilderness, 1975.

Photo credit: Tom Jones. Used by permission of the photographer.

We played a part

After those talks in 2015, I took time to read online what popular history had to say about Suharto, Lim Bian Kee, and the New Order government. A few paragraphs covered the outrages of the coup. The *tapols* were barely mentioned. Nothing about what led to Jakarta's sudden U-turn from *Bapreru* to releasing everyone. None of the adjectives normally attached to the memory of a monster in Suharto's profile.

It struck me there is a kind of symmetry to what is left out of the popular record about the perpetrators of Indonesia's long night of repression and the empty page of history that ought to be set aside to honor Huang Wen-Hsien and the ingenious strategy he crafted that helped so many survive and regain their freedom, who might otherwise have perished on Buru Island.

I knew Huang well enough to know he would be embarrassed by such an encomium. He would surely remind me of the many strands in that "skein of causality" that were not of his making. That is wise, of course, as Huang was wise, but it takes nothing away from his achievement.

We played a part. I believe our strand was crucial to the skein, our work essential to the outcome. Without domestic pressure for change within Indonesia, however, without global outcry about the occupation of East Timor that saddled Jakarta with one too many outrages to try and justify, without the visionary leadership in Congress of Don Fraser, the whisperings of Benni Moerdani, and who knows what other factors we knew nothing about, our efforts, however ingenious, however relentless, could not have brought the *tapols* home.

But without the campaign, what was to stop the *Bapreru* plan from becoming Jakarta's Final Solution, to be carried out behind the same wall of silence and international complicity that had stood so long? Without the campaign, would the *tapols* ever have come home?

What mattered to Huang, I know, was that they did come home. I think, just the same, a glimmer of their freedom and of the ordinary joys they share each day belonged to Huang Wen-Hsien, to bequeath to his sons and their children and to those of us who, because of his work, had a chance to be part of a human rights struggle that had at least 35,000 happy endings, and perhaps many more. If there is a richer reward to be found in this world, Huang didn't need it, and neither do I.

9

A promise to the teacher: *Al-Ustadh* Mahmoud Mohamed Taha of Sudan

The age-old dream of the human caravan is not to send astronauts in their orbit in outer space... it is to send its individuals—every single individual in his orbit of self-realization. It is high time that this dream be thus reinterpreted. It is also the sacred duty of every man and woman to help intelligently reorientate human endeavour towards the culmination of this pilgrimage.

—Mahmoud Muhammad Taha—Answers to the questions of Mr John Voll—July 17, 1963

A conversation in Khartoum

In 2007, on a blistering July afternoon in Khartoum, my friend and host Albaqir Mukhtar Alafif and I left Sharg El-Neil College and the conference on Poverty and Security that was the occasion for my visit, and took in the sights: palm trees along the Nile; a smattering of high-rise buildings among countless adobe homes and small markets along the road where women shopped and chatted in their *tobs* of dazzling colors while men in traditional *jallabiyas* or khaki trousers and loose-fitting shirts drank tea, argued, and laughed.

"This isn't Basil Dearden's *Khartoum*," I reflected, recalling the lavish 1966 epic that starred Laurence Olivier as the Mahdi. "Somebody ought to make a film that tells Sudan's real story." Albaqir listened while I bemoaned the inauthenticity of the movie's depiction of history, asking why no one had made a more accurate biopic about the Mahdi, a towering nineteenth century figure who led Sudan's struggle for independence. "Perhaps that story is no longer so important," he said. "There is, however, a story from Sudan that everyone on Earth should know. It is the story of *Al-Ustadh* Mahmoud Mohamed Taha."

Mahmoud Mohamed Taha.

Photo credit: Shaykh Omer; public domain.

Although the name Taha was immediately familiar to me, I couldn't exactly remember why. I asked Albaqir about him, and as he replied, memories from more than 20 years ago came back into clear focus. Albaqir dropped me at my room just before sunset. He told me he would seek an invitation for me to join him the next evening at the home of Abdel Lateef, whom I had met at the conference. Abdel Lateef was a senior leader of the movement that Taha had created during his lifetime, a group known as *Jamhurieen*, or in English, the Republican Brothers and Sisters of Sudan.

Alone that night, I pieced together what Albaqir had just told me and what I had learned long ago about Mahmoud Mohamed Taha, known by his followers as *al-Ustadh*, meaning "esteemed teacher". As I did, the inspiration I felt decades before when I campaigned for Taha's release from prison and joined the later efforts to stop his execution was reawakened in me.

The next evening, at Abdel Lateef's home, about 100 members of the movement gathered for a prayer service. As the verses and prayers were chanted under the stars, Abdel Lateef, watching me take it all in, often smiled. The chanting, known as *inshad*, was hauntingly beautiful and uplifting. It was possible to feel the unity and devotion of the *Jamhurieen*, and also, in a way I cannot adequately express, the almost palpable presence of Taha's spirit. I found myself making a promise to that spiritual presence: if I could find a way to bring his story to the world, I would do everything I could to accomplish it. With this inspiration, I presented Albaqir's idea of taking Taha's story to people I knew in Hollywood. The suggestion was enthusiastically embraced by nearly everyone. Before we dispersed, Abdel Lateef told the gathering in Arabic that he often worried when outsiders attended because their presence could affect the peace of *Jamhurieen* gatherings. But he added, "Mr. David has brought his own peace." Albaqir quietly translated the words for me. "This is his blessing," he whispered.

Taha is adopted by Amnesty as a prisoner of conscience

Once more back in my room, I began following the breadcrumbs of memory back to my first acquaintance with Taha's epic story, which had begun, for me, more than 20 years ago. In 1983, about a year into my tenure as western region director of Amnesty International USA, I had received an alert from Amnesty's Urgent Action Network that Muslim teacher and reformer Mahmoud Mohamed Taha had been arrested in Sudan.

Taha was an important figure in the history of his country, first in its struggle for independence from British colonial rule, then as the leader of a movement for human rights, equality, and peace. He wrote books and pamphlets about what he called "true Islam". His movement advocated and practiced his compassionate interpretation of the faith. Its principles included tolerance of other religions, peaceful coexistence with Israel, equal rights for women, reform of Sharia law to protect human rights, and strict adherence to nonviolence.

The Muslim Brotherhood, a powerful political force in Sudan, tried him for apostasy in 1968 but at that time had no authority to carry out a sentence. But when the Gafaar Nimeiri dictatorship announced in 1982 its intention to impose Sharia on all of Sudan, including the Christian and Animist majority in the South, Taha's vocal protest intensified Nimeiri's antagonism against him and his followers. In the spring of 1983, a few months before promulgating and enforcing the new laws, the regime arrested Taha.

Amnesty International immediately adopted Taha and dozens of his followers who were arrested at the same time, including his daughters Asma and Sumaya, as prisoners of conscience and issued the first of three successive Urgent Action appeals to generate international pressure on the regime for their release. Scott Harrison and Ellen Moore, who ran Amnesty USA's Urgent Action Network out of their home in Colorado, immediately recognized the importance of the case and circulated it both widely and strategically. Over the next 18 months, our office publicized Taha's story in the LA media.

In 1984 we featured Taha's case on *Amnesty International Reports*, a monthly show on the National Public Radio (NPR) Santa Monica affiliate KCRW. The show was the brainchild of Ruth Seymour, the station's brilliant and visionary general manager. Each month on a Friday during lunch hour drive time, Ruth interviewed me about three countries in the news, ending with publicity of a featured case. Listeners were invited to phone the station to request a summary of the case that included officials' names and addresses for letters and telegrams.

The show was syndicated to 20 NPR stations in the USA and 25 more worldwide. A featured case usually prompted 300 to as many as 800 intercessions from Los Angeles-area listeners alone. The Taha case inspired over 1,600 local calls, an unprecedented response that was never equaled in the five years of the program's run.

Worldwide, appeals for Taha certainly numbered in the tens of thousands, amplifying domestic outcry in Sudan at a time of sweeping unrest. Taha's imprisonment had outraged many in Sudan, a country with a tradition of political pluralism and tolerance. Food and fuel shortages were driving more and more people into the streets, demanding change. The protests would grow into an uprising remarkably like the revolution that recently toppled Omar Bashir.

Taha is released, but does not fall silent

At the end of November 1984, Taha and all of his followers were released. Jubilation greeted his freedom in Khartoum and in LA, but it was short-lived. Taha immediately published a pamphlet, "Either This or the Flood" condemning the amputations, floggings, and other human rights abuses inflicted on the Sudanese people in the wake of the so-called "Islamic Laws" of 1983. Citing the Qur'anic verse, "There is no compulsion in religion," Taha called the policies a distortion of Islam and a tool to humiliate and oppress the people. He pointed out the danger to national unity created by the laws, warning of another civil war. Taha was re-arrested in January 1985. A show trial was held at which the pamphlet was the sole piece of evidence. A single judge, a member of the Muslim Brotherhood, condemned Taha to death. He was executed on January 18, 1985. Outrage over his public hanging fueled the growing protest movement. After months of demonstrations, the Nimeiri regime fell without a shot fired. For four remarkable years, democracy returned to Sudan. Taha's daughter Asma, now an attorney, filed suit against the government, successfully demanding annulment of her father's death sentence. Shock at the execution spread internationally. The Arab Human Rights Association declared January 18 "Arab Human Rights Day". The magazine *Jeune Afrique* deplored the act as a crime and called Taha "Sudan's Gandhi".

Keeping my promise

In 2007, reflecting on the promise I had made in Abdel Lateef's home, I began to consider how to keep it. It had been many years, but along the way, I renewed some acquaintances, like writer-director Paul Haggis, through work I had done with Paul's help during a 1990 displacement crisis in Sudan, on behalf of the US Committee for Refugees. I had great confidence in the ability of my longtime Amnesty International publicist and dear friend Judy Martinez to connect with Paul and other industry friends. For eight years in the 1980s, Judy Martinez, as media director for the western region, had created unprecedented opportunities for Amnesty in the entertainment community. Using her consummate ability as a publicist and event producer, Judy led the way on one successful event after another for Amnesty in Hollywood while placing me on an endless stream of radio and TV interview shows to build the organization's previously negligible profile in Los Angeles.

Judy Martinez, second from right, with, from left, John Huston, Kris Kristofferson, and Argentinian former prisoner of conscience Alicia Partnoy, at Amnesty's 25th anniversary Gala in Los Angeles, 1986.

Photo credit: Mitzi Trumbo, used by permission of the photographer.

Judy's work was and is a model of collaboration and networking, distinguished above all by consistently providing opportunities for industry leaders to do real human rights work, not just make appearances. The intercession on behalf of Carla Cristi, remembered here in an earlier chapter, was one of countless occasions when this activism made a difference not only for the cause but also for real human beings in peril.

So I turned to Judy first. We agreed Paul Haggis was the right screenwriter to talk to about developing a screenplay, and the occasion for that conversation soon appeared. While I was back at Amnesty USA in an interim role under then executive director

Larry Cox, at my suggestion Judy was brought on to produce a high-profile event in Los Angeles as part of Amnesty's world-wide campaign to shut down Guantanamo in 2008. We asked celebrities to don orange prison suits and be photographed in a replica of the Guantanamo prison cell. Judy reached out widely and delivered a remarkable media event on the Santa Monica Promenade, with Larry Cox, as always brilliant at the microphone. The brave voices that risked incurring the wrath of the Patriot Act administration to stand with us: Martin Sheen, Mark Ruffalo, and Paul Haggis.

Paul Haggis's involvement created the opportunity to discuss the Taha project with him. At a Santa Monica coffee shop over break-fast, while waiting for Judy to make it in from South Pasadena, I related the story to Paul and his then-wife Deborah. Paul was gen-uinely interested. Deborah loved the idea of honoring a Muslim leader who practiced and preached equal rights for women. Paul invited me to prepare a treatment, a kind of narrative outline of the story. It took two years to prepare a treatment of some 150 pages. I started with a biography, *Islam's Perfect Stranger,* drawing freely upon the then-unpublished manuscript with the enthusi-astic support of author Edward Thomas of the UK.

I eventually discussed the project with Prof. Abdullahi An-Na'im, whom I have known since 1986. He was one of Taha's students and his translator. He became one of the world's foremost experts on human rights and Islamic law and a principal exponent of the ideas Taha taught, struggled and sacrificed everything for during his lifetime. Abdullahi told me about Ernest Johnson, known in the movement as Abdalla Al-Ameriki, and suggested I contact him. This introduction helped me find my way to make the story accessible to Americans.

My friend Mike Keplinger, a skilled photographer, hosted a visit to Seattle in 2009 and filmed over four hours of interviews with Ernest for me so I could study them at home. A few months later, Ernest and I went to Iowa City to interview *Jamhurieen*, many of whom resettled there in the aftermath of Taha's execution. More filmed interviews conducted there were rich in anecdotes that became scenes in the treatment and eventually the script.

Dr Ernest Johnson speaking at a sit-in at the University of Hawaii in 1975.

Photographer unknown; used by permission of Dr Johnson.

Producer Marc Levey agreed to represent the project after Paul Haggis's production company was unable to do it. Marc and I had worked together while I was back at Amnesty in 2008. Over the ensuing years, he introduced the project to colleagues and contacts at the Producers Guild of America and to Lionsgate, Participant Media, Netflix, and others in the industry. It eventually became inescapably apparent that no other production company would consider the project based on a treatment alone. So, with irreplaceable assistance from script consultant Jacqueline Dollard, whom Judy Martinez had recruited to help, from 2014 to 2018, I crafted a screenplay.

A turning point

Once the first draft was completed in 2018, in an effort to bring the story to life for our friends in Hollywood, Judy Martinez and I organized a visit to Los Angeles for Taha's daughter Asma. Also joining us was Emory University Professor Abdullahi An-Na'im, who, on the final day of the visit, delivered a powerful lecture to a rapt audience of faculty and students at Loyola Marymount University (LMU). His address and his equally stirring responses to questions created a reflective glow on everyone, our small group most of all.

Ernest Johnson, who had come down from Seattle to join us, came with Asma, my wife Tina and me to hear Abdullahi speak and to answer questions about the project, its history and aspirations. Afterwards, on the short drive back from LMU to Venice, where our guests were staying, all of us were hungry and tired but also so stimulated by Abdullahi's presentation that nobody wanted the evening to end. At about ten p.m. on this last evening together, we did not want to settle for something ordinary in one of the great restaurant towns in the country. Yet we could find nothing open. And suddenly there it was, on Lincoln between Marina Del Rey and Venice, the proverbial International House of Pancakes. Driving, I muttered sheepishly, "Well, IHOP is open." I expected silence if not groans or laughter. I think Tina did giggle. But Ernest decided the matter. "Oh, I can eat pancakes at any hour," he said. I could hear the smile. And all of a sudden, there we were together around a tiny table, alone in the place but for a handful of other nighthawks, all beholden to one sleepy-eyed server and in no hurry themselves. I didn't have to look at the menu. Breakfast out for me, whatever the hour, is two eggs over easy, hash browns, and ham or bacon, wheat toast, milk, and orange juice. In deference to our Muslim friends, I skipped the swine that night, substituting a small steak. My likeness does not appear next to the word "unpredictable" in any dictionary.

Asma Mahmoud Mohamed Taha at Loyola Marymount University in 2018.

Photo credit: Margaret Molloy, used by permission of the photographer.

The advantage of this lack of culinary imagination or curiosity is being able to watch the faces of those in my company, each one searching the laminated pages of the menu for inspiration, Tina most of all, because she reads a menu as if her life hangs in the balance. I have always loved these moments, never more than on that evening at IHOP. Ernest made his comments and suggestions in Arabic, to appreciative smiles and soft laughter from

Asma and Abdullahi. These are dear friends of many, many years, I reflected, their bonds forged in struggle, in prison, through revolution, and in shared purpose. Together after many years apart, taking up where they left off as if no time had passed, as all dear friends do.

Even in great pain, just weeks before hip surgery, Abdullahi's lively eyes sparkled as he laughed. Asma's too, little beacons of irrepressible joy. Tina, of course, fit right in. I looked from face to face and saw that Ernest was doing the same. "This is like a movie," he said. And it was, although I can't say how exactly. Our long endeavor had reached a kind of crest of possibility, and it seemed to all of us, I think, that this was our momentary opportunity to share that feeling. The pancakes came. Laughter and quiet chatter gave way to savoring blueberries, waffles, maple syrup, and coffee. The quiet too seemed a blessing, but then everything seems a blessing in such company. Somewhere between the words, the dining together, and the closeness enforced by the undersized table, we felt in common that sense of pausing at a crossroads, with great changes just ahead.

That feeling that our endeavor had reached a turning point was prescient. But the year that followed unfolded in ways we could never have predicted. A few months after that evening, Asma was back in prison in Khartoum as the uprising that later toppled Omar Bashir grew into a peaceful revolution. Her leadership led to her repeated detention. Then, with her release from prison, it seemed like a promising new chapter had begun with Sudan's return to democracy in the summer of 2019.

The fragility of Sudan's revolution has been tragically revealed as civil war has now broken out between opposing factions of the military and paramilitary commanders. The resulting devastation has now forced the mass dislocation of millions of Sudanese, and at the time of writing, there is no end in sight.

For the movie project, our common intuition that night at IHOP turned out to be prescient in another way. During the preparation for our event at LMU that evening, our host, Prof. Amir Hussain, suggested I discuss the project with the executive director of the Muslim Public Affairs Council of Los Angeles (MPAC), Salam al-Marayati. Amir set up a meeting for me, and it proved to be the breakthrough we'd been searching for.

A crucial boost from the Muslim Public Affairs Council of Los Angeles

Salam was a supremely gracious host. He shared with me that MPAC's founder, Dr Maher Hathout, a pioneer in Muslim institution building, deeply admired Mahmoud Mohamed Taha, regarding him as a personal inspiration. Salam had learned of Taha from Dr Hathout and told me, "All things Taha are close to my heart. What can I do?"

"We have a script, but it has far to go. I need to expose it to a Muslim screenwriter, most of all for an assessment of its authenticity and sensitivity with respect to culture. Ideally, a Sudanese."

Salam introduced me at once to Suhan (Sue) Obeidi, director of MPAC's Hollywood Bureau. We talked over all the challenges we faced. Sue offered to post an announcement about our project to MPAC's network of Muslim screenwriters, inviting anyone interested to read the script and offer notes. The response was overwhelming. Of the 24 screenwriters, all of them women, who expressed interest; of them, 12 read the script and of those, 6 submitted notes and raised questions. Every set of notes was valuable, but one set was exceptionally incisive, revealing, and course correcting. The screenwriter who submitted them was Issraa El-Kogali Häggström.

Breakthrough!

Issraa was born in Khartoum and raised in the UK, US, Egypt, and Sudan. She now lives with her husband and two children in Stockholm. She is the great-great-granddaughter of Mohamed Ahmed Al-Mahdi, whose nationalist movement was depicted in the movie *Khartoum* in a way that had so outraged and disappointed me, as I related at the beginning of this chapter. A founding member of Sudan Film Factory, Issraa recently rose to prominence as co-producer, with Amjad Abu Alala (*You Will Die at Twenty* [2020]) of the first Sudanese film ever exhibited in competition at Cannes, *Goodbye Julia*. The film, directed by Mohamed Kordofani, won the Freedom Prize in the prestigious *Un Certain Regard* category.

Issraa El-Kogali Häggström on the red carpet for the exhibition of *Goodbye Julia*, 2023.

After providing her assistance with the screenplay, and even though she was busy with *Goodbye Julia*, in 2021 Issraa agreed to co-produce the Taha film, now under the title *The Second Message*. Subsequently, after prayer and reflection, she agreed to take the helm as director. Breakthrough! Thank you, Amir Hussain, Salam al-Marayati, and Sue Obeidi. Or, as I remember saying often in Khartoum, *Shukran jazeelan!*

Thanks to MPAC's announcement, Issraa's arrival, and Judy's expert communications management, *The Second Message* now has a chance to be part of the historic twenty-first-century flowering of Sudanese cinema. Although filmmaking in Sudan has been made impossible by the civil war and its devastation, the foundation laid by Amjad Abu Alala, Mohamed Kordofani, and their luminous films offers hope for an unlimited future.

Very often in my long career, I have found that people are moved to act in solidarity and shared struggle not so much by being exposed to facts, statistics, and analysis, but by hearing a story of people who stand up to oppression and tyranny no matter the cost, and by learning ways to stand with them.

I am honored and humbled to have been given the responsibility to bring this story to those who can tell it to the world. With Issraa's leadership, I am now increasingly confident that the story of *al-Ustadh* Mahmoud Mohamed Taha's epic life and inspiring personal example will reach a global audience through the magic of cinema. When that day comes, I want all of us to get back to that IHOP, fill up the tables, stay late into the night, and invite all the nighthawks who wander in to enjoy a stack of hot pancakes and a cup of coffee with us. May the day come soon, God willing, or, as my friends say, *Inshallah*.

Glossary

activism: the policy or action of using vigorous campaigning to bring about political or social change (Oxford Languages)

apartheid: first used in 1929; abolished in 1994 (South Africa); a policy or system of segregation or discrimination on grounds of race (OED)

civil disobedience: the refusal to obey the demands or commands of a government or occupying power, without resorting to violence or active measures of opposition (Britannica)

executive clemency: the power of the president or a governor to pardon, commute, or reduce the sentence of a person convicted of or facing prosecution for a criminal offense (Long Island Institute)

fascism: first used in 1915 (Italy); an authoritarian and right-wing form of government and social organization (Oxford Reference)

human rights: first used in reference to a cause in 1831 (USA, Garrison); rights believed to belong justifiably to every person (Oxford Languages)

Indigenous people(s): first used by the United Nations in 2002; First Nation people or tribal groups; a much-criticized term not yet replaced in international usage (Wikipedia)

*jallabiya***:** a loose-fitting traditional men's outer garment from the Nile Valley (Wikipedia)

Jim Crow laws: first used in 1864; in effect until 1965 (US); state and local laws introduced in the Southern United States in the late nineteenth and early twentieth centuries that enforced racial segregation (Wikipedia)

movement: a collective attempt by a large group of people to change government policy or social values (Wikipedia)

solidarity: first used in 1660 (Locke); support for one group of people by another; unity (OED)

struggle: a hard fight in which people try to obtain or achieve something, especially something that somebody else does not want them to have (OED)

tob: the Sudanese national dress for women, a long piece of cloth wrapped around the body and looped over the head and tossed over the right shoulder (Wikipedia)

Appendix 1

Chronology of the author's involvement in Amnesty International

1973   Recruited by Joan Baez and Ginetta Sagan while teaching junior high school in the San Francisco Bay Area; organized local chapters throughout Northern California

1974   Approved by Amnesty researcher Huang Wen-Hsien as Indonesia Country Coordination Director for Amnesty USA

1975   Elected to the board of directors of Amnesty USA; served until 1982

1976   Delegated to Amnesty development conference in Gotemba, Japan

1977   Coordinated the Campaign for Long-Term Prisoners in Indonesia for Amnesty USA

1978   Elected chairperson of Amnesty USA's board of directors; served until 1980

1979   Delegated to a strategy and planning retreat of death penalty abolitionists in Tennessee

1979   Delegated to support legal defense teams trying to stop executions in Florida and Georgia

1981   Delegated to support the legal defense team trying to prevent an execution in Louisiana

1981   Elected chairperson of Amnesty International's International Council Meeting in Montreal, Canada; reelected in 1982, 1983, 1985 (when meetings became biennial)

1982   Appointed Western Region Director of Amnesty USA; served until 1990

1984   Delegated to Amnesty development conference in Arusha, Tanzania

1985   Appointed chairperson of Amnesty's Committee on Long-Range Organizational Development; delivered its report to the 1987 International Council Meeting held near Campinas, Brazil

1990   Over the next three years, spoke at over 20 colleges and universities in the US and Canada at the invitation of Amnesty chapters on campus about challenges facing the movement

2007   Appointed interim Head of Regions for Amnesty USA; promoted to interim Department Head for Membership and Campaigns; served until 2008

2011   In a "full circle" moment, chosen by Executive Director Larry Cox to present to Joan Baez the first-ever Joan Baez Award for Human Rights Activism at Amnesty USA's fiftieth anniversary gathering in San Francisco

Appendix 2

Nongovernmental, intergovernmental and other organizations

American Civil Liberties Union (ACLU): www.aclu.org

Amnesty International: www.amnesty.org

Amnesty International USA: www.amnestyusa.org

California Appellate Project: www.capsf.org

Committee for Human Rights in North Korea: www.hrnk.org

Cultural Survival: www.culturalsurvival.org

Death Penalty Action: www.deathpenaltyaction.org

Death Penalty Focus: www.deathpenalty.org

Death Penalty Information Center: www.deathpenaltyinfo.org

Forest Peoples Programme: www.forestpeoples.org

Human Rights Watch: www.hrw.org

Inter-American Commission on Human Rights: www.oas.org

International Commission of Jurists: www.icj.org

International Committee of the Red Cross: www.icrc.org

Muslim Public Affairs Council of Los Angeles: www.mpac.org

Rainforest Foundation: www.rainforestfoundation.org

Rainforest Fund: www.rainforestfund.org

Survival International: www.survivalinternational.org

United Farm Workers: www.ufw.org

United Nations High Commissioner for Refugees: www.unhcr.org

US Committee for Refugees: www.refugees.org

Recommended projects

- Chapter One: (racism)

  View Ava DuVernay's documentary *Origin*, based on Isabel Wilkerson's groundbreaking 2020 book *Caste: The Origins of Our Discontents*. Identify any implications of the film for your perspective on racism.

- Chapters Two and Three: (the death penalty)

  Assign or undertake a study on one or both of these topics: Race and the Death Penalty, The Death Penalty and Innocence; use the 2024 Marcellus Williams (Missouri) and/or the 2011 Troy Davis (Georgia) cases as points of concentration for the study.

- Chapter Six: (Fascism)

  Assign or undertake a study paper or report on fascism in the twenty-first century. Include evaluations of the application of the term to current trends and political factions in the US, Europe, and Latin America.

- Chapter Nine: (Sudan, film)

  Assign or undertake an examination of the current blossoming of Sudanese cinema; include viewings of *You Will Die at Twenty*, directed by Amjad Abu Alala, and/or *Goodbye Julia* directed by Mohamed Kordofani. Include consideration of the prospects for Sudanese cinema's future in light of the ongoing civil war in Sudan.

Bibliography

Allende, S. (1973). In These Times, 'Salvador Allende's Final Speech on Sept. 11, 1973', September 11, 2017: Chicago, IL.

Almanac Singers, The (1941). 'Which Side Are You On', *Talking Union* [Vinyl] New York: Keynote Records.

Amnesty International. (2023). *Civil Disobedience Tool Kit.* Amnesty International Publications: London, UK. Access online at: www.amnesty.org/fr/wp content/uploads/2024/02/ACT1074712024ENGLISH.pdf

Amnesty International. (2007). *Maze of Injustice: The failure to protect Indigenous women from sexual violence in the USA.* Amnesty International publications: London, UK. Access at: https://www.amnesty.org/fr/wp-content/uploads/2021/05/AMR510352007ENGLISH.pdf

Arens, R. (1976). *Genocide in Paraguay.* Temple University Press: Philadelphia, PA.

Baez, J. (1964). 'Oh Freedom', *Joan Baez: The First Lady of Folk 1958 - 1961* [Vinyl] London: Jasmine Records.

Congressional Record: *Long-term Imprisonment Without Trial in Indonesia: Hearings before the Subcommittee on International Organizations of the Committee on International Relations, United States House of Representatives, October 18, 1977.*

Dorfman, A. (2011). 'Novelist-playwright Ariel Dorfman'. Interview on The Tavis Smiley Show, www.pbs.org, New York: November 1, 2011.

Dorfman, A. (1999). *Heading South, Looking North.* Norton Paperback: New York City, NY.

Evans, M. (2022). 'Lilian Ngoyi: an heroic South African woman whose story hasn't been fully told.' The Conversation: Cape Town, South Africa.

Goldman, E. (1931). *Living My Life*. Alfred A. Knopf: New York City, NY. (in-text quote is from a passage on p.56).

Goodbye Julia (2023). Directed by Kordofani, M. [Film]. Amjad Abu Alala Productions: Dubai, UAE.

Grahame, K. (1908). *The Wind in the Willows*. Charles Scribner's Sons: New York City, NY.

Harris, E. (1979). 'Hickory Wind', *Blue Kentucky Girl* [Vinyl] New York: Nonesuch Records.

Hawk, D. (2012). Second Edition. *The Hidden Gulag: The Lives and Voices of "Those Who are Sent to the Mountains."* A report published by the Committee for Human Rights in North Korea: Washington, D.C.

Himmler, H. (1943). 'Speech to SS Officers in Posen'. Excerpted in Moeller, R. (2009) *The Nazi State and German Society: A Brief History with Documents* (the Bedford Series in His.) Bedford/St. Martin's: Boston, MA. Pg.139–140.

Huang, W. (1977). *Long-Term Imprisonment without Trial in Indonesia*. Amnesty International publications: London, UK.

I Love Lucy, (1951–1957) [Television]. Desilu Productions: Los Angeles, CA.

Jassin, H.B. (1955). *Kesusasteraan Indonesia Modern dalam Kritik dan Essay*. Gunung Agung: Jakarta, Indonesia. Includes the uncredited photo of Pramoedya Ananta Toer used here.

Jealous, B. (2016). 'California Voters Should Remember Troy Davis This November', access at: www.huffingtonpost.com, September 20, 2016.

Jeune Afrique magazine, 'A Crime: Mahmoud Mohamed Taha is hanged for his beliefs.' January 29, 1985 (cover story). Paris, France.

Kim, D. (2004). *The 21st century and the Korean people: selected speeches of Kim Dae-jung, 1998-2004*. Hakgojae Publishing: Seoul, South Korea.

La Boheme (1896). Puccini, G. Composer, Illica, L., Giacosa, G. Librettists, [Opera] from Murger, H. *Scènes de la vie de bohème* (1851).

La Strada, (1954). Directed by Fellini, F. [Film]. Ponti-De Laurentiis Cinematografica: Venice, Italy.

Longfellow, H.W. (1863). *Tales of a Wayside Inn*. Original publisher unknown, available on Kindle.

Madama Butterfly (1904). Puccini, G. Composer, Illica, L., Giacosa, G. Libettists, based on Long, J. *Madame Butterfly* (1898), dramatized by Belasco, D, *Madame Butterfly: A Tragedy of Japan* (1900).

New York Times Book Review (2020). "Isabel Wilkerson's 'Caste' Is an 'Instant American Classic' About Our Abiding Sin", Dwight Garner, July 31, 2020, updated Jan. 21, 2021. New York City, NY.

New York Times Editorial (1978). 'Amnesty's Odd Man In', December 14, 1978. New York City, NY.

New York Times Op Ed (1978). byline: "A South African". 'It Is Not God Who Made Apartheid', May 6, 1978. New York City, NY.

Nights of Cabiria, (1957). Directed by Fellini, F. [Film]. Dino De Laurentiis: Venice, Italy.

Origin, (2023). Directed by DuVernay, A. [Film]. Paul Games and Ava DuVernay, ARRAY Filmworks: Los Angeles, CA, USA.

Parra, V. (1966). 'Gracias a la Vida', *Las Últimas Composiciones* [Vinyl] New York: RCA Victor.

Phantom of the Opera (1925). Directed by Julian, R. [Film]. Universal Pictures: Los Angeles, CA.

Smiley, T. (2011). *Novelist Playwright Ariel Dorfman: The Tavis Smiley Show*. [Television]. New York City, New York: Public Broadcasting Service (PBS) www.pbs.org, Nov. 1, 2011.

Taha, M. author, An-Na'im, A. translator (1987). *The Second Message of Islam*. Syracuse University Press: Syracuse, NY.

Thomas, E. (2010). *Islam's Perfect Stranger: The Life of Mahmud Muhammad Taha, Muslim Reformer of Sudan*. I.B. Tauris & Co. Ltd.: London, UK.

Toer, P. (1988). *The Mute's Soliloquy*. Penguin Books: New York City, NY.

Tosca (1900). Puccini, G. Composer, Illica, L., Giacosa, G. Librettists, from Sardou, V. *La Tosca* (1887).

Turandot (1926). Puccini, G. Composer, Adami, G., Simoni, R. Librettists, from Gozzi, C. *Turandot* (1762).

White, E.B. (1952). *Charlotte's Web*. Harper & Brothers: New York City, NY.

You Will Die at Twenty (2020). Directed by A. Alala [Film]. Amjad Abu Alala Productions: Dubai, UAE.

Recommended further reading

- Chapter One: (racism)

  "Isabel Wilkerson's 'Caste' Is an 'Instant American Classic' About Our Abiding Sin", Book Review by Dwight Garner, *New York Times*, July 31, 2020, updated Jan. 21, 2021. New York City, NY.

- Chapter Four: (Lilian Ngoyi, civil disobedience)

  New York Times Op-Ed, (1978), "It Is Not God Who Made Apartheid", byline "A South African"; letters of Lilian Ngoyi published anonymously.

  Amnesty International's online Civil Disobedience Tool Kit; access at:

  www.amnesty.org/fr/wpcontent/uploads/2024/02/ACT10 74712024ENGLISH.pdf

- Chapter Five: (First Nation/Indigenous peoples)

  Amnesty International. (2007) *Maze of injustice: The failure to protect Indigenous women from sexual violence in the USA.* Amnesty International Publications: London, UK.

  The 2007 report along with its campaign outcomes (updated as recently as 2022) can be found in these links: https:// www.amnesty.org/fr/wpcontent/uploads/2021/05/AMR5 10352007ENGLISH.pdfhttps://www.amnestyusa.org/press-releases/usa-amnesty-international-commends-president-obama-for-signing-tribal-law-and-order-act/%22"

- Chapter Seven: (North Korea)

Hawk, D. (2012). *The Hidden Gulag: The Lives and Voices of "Those Who are Sent to the Mountains"*, second edition. A report published by the Committee for Human Rights in North Korea: Washington, D.C. Access at: www.hrnk.org/uplo ads/pdfs/HRNK_HiddenGulag2_Web_5-18.pdf

Index

www.ingramcontent.com/pod-product-compliance
Lightning Source LLC
Chambersburg PA
CBHW070711280326
41926CB00089B/3985

* 9 7 8 1 9 1 6 9 8 5 9 3 3 *